# Counseling Families

*From Insight
to Intervention*

# Counseling
# Families

## James P. Osterhaus

**Ministry
Resources
Library**

Zondervan Publishing House • Grand Rapids, MI

Edited by Joan Johnson
Designed by Louise Bauer and James E. Ruark

Library of Congress Cataloging in Publication Data

Osterhaus, James P.
   Counseling families : from insight to intervention / James P. Osterhaus.
      p.   cm.
   Includes bibliographical references.
   ISBN 0-310-43780-6
   1. Church work with families. 2. Family psychotherapy. I. Title.
BV4438.O88      1989                                              89-38051
259'.1—dc20                                                        CIP

Printed in the United States of America

89   90   91   92   93   94 / AF / 10   9   9   8   7   6   5   4   3   2   1

*To my wife Marcy,*
*My constant source of encouragement*

# Contents

# Acknowledgments

Books are best written when the author is surrounded by friends. I have been blessed by an abundance of them in my lifetime and during this project have called on many friends for assistance—directly, in the actual framing and writing of ideas; and indirectly, for support and encouragement.

My greatest friend in life has been my wife, Marcy, whose loyalty and encouragement have seen me through many projects in the last twenty years. My children have also been most patient and supportive.

Two men have helped me significantly to understand and articulate the ideas in this book. I have also been honored to work with each of them as partners. Joe Jurkowski and Rich Eberly continue to work professionally as counselors in Virginia.

A number of people were very helpful in editing this manuscript. My deepest thanks to Dick Busby, who was my final editor. My dear friends Steve and Peggy Noll, Dan Williamson, Ron Jenkins, Mike Henning, and Ron Davis all read the manuscript and offered invaluable comments and assistance.

# Foreword

It is extremely rare, unfortunately, to discover within the contemporary Christian community a person who uses the best of theological and psychological insight in order to become a channel of healing grace for hurting families. Dr. James Osterhaus is such a person. Jim's deep commitment to Jesus Christ couple with his ability to integrate biblical and psychological truth has enabled him to become a uniquely gifted counselor.

The scores of testimonies shared with me by previously fractured families and broken individuals further validates Jim's counseling skills. Beyond his outstanding academic accouterments there is a heart that pulsates for people in need.

In this, his first book, Dr. Osterhaus tracks new territory in helping us to understand how relationships in general and family units in particular truly function. Sharing from his rich and diverse background as a clinical psychologist, family therapist, and counseling center director, Jim gives to the reader both personal illustrations of families working through crises and personal exercises that can be helpful to all of us in our homes and vocations.

Quoting from such diverse sources as Jonathan Edwards and David Elkind, Jim offers a book that is easily readable and understandable without ever falling into the trap of becoming simplistic. In his carving out new territory, my hope is that *Counseling Families* will be widely received both as a textbook in schools of theology and psychology and among lay readers who want to grow in their understanding of relationships and families. I highly recommend this creative new work by an outstanding psychologist to all who seek to become whole in Christ and in their interactions with others.

*Ron Davis*
Senior Pastor
Community Presbyterian Church
Danville, California

# Preface

Life pulsates with relationships. We live in families, work in organizations, congregate in churches, shop in groups, and generally spend most of our time in and out of relationships.

But many of us don't notice this. In our culture we emphasize the individual. We focus on the trees and ignore the forest. This also happens when we read the Bible, which is primarily a relational book. As we read Scripture, we tend to overlook the inherent drama of relationships. There is much to learn, however, in concentrating on the dynamics of relationships.

Crucial relationships are sustained by fragile links. The focus of a relationship is much different from that of the individual. Relational focus demands wholeness. The family seen together is different from the family members seen separately. Actually the family cannot be adequately understood even when each person in the family is analyzed. Each member is shaped by and dependent on every other person in the family.

Relationships in families are critical, but we must not swing the pendulum too far into relational considerations or we will neglect the individual. If we are to counsel effectively, we must understand the individual and his responsibilities as well as his relationships.

This book is designed to help us understand relationships. It is about counseling, communication, and change. My goal is threefold: to explain phenomena within relationships, to examine the organization and function of relationships, and to identify ways to change relationships if they go awry. I have chosen to emphasize the family, God's primary organizational unit, as I pursue these goals.

*Counseling Families* is divided into two sections. The first sets the foundation. It shows how we perceive the world and formulate reality with the two sides of the brain. Thinking about relationships will require new ways of attending to information. We will see that gathering the relevant information about relationships requires some skills that are unfamiliar to many of us.

We will also see how communication is the adhesive that holds relationships together. It is imperative that communication be understood and handled with care.

The second section describes how the family functions and how problems develop. The family as seen as a dynamic whole unit develops over time and passes through various predictable stages in which the members must confront and successfully negotiate certain distinct tasks. Problems develop in families at times when things that are supposed to happen don't, or when things that aren't supposed to happen do.

As time passes, a family must maintain continuity while confronting constant demands to change. The family develops a particular structure, which can be identified as it carries on its business. Problems can develop in this structure.

My hope is that upon completing this book, you will appreciate the intricacies of relationships and understand how such intricacies affect your lives. I hope also to give you tools to enable you to mend broken relationships.

# Part 1
# FOUNDATIONS

# 1
# Perceiving

I ushered the mother and father and fourteen-year-old boy into my office. The well-dressed mother appeared somewhat ill at ease. The father sat rigidly in his chair; though he was obviously uncomfortable, he maintained his composure with precision. The boy, wearing T-shirt, jeans, and sneakers, looked like most teenage boys—informal but neat. He seemed disinterested.

I greeted everyone warmly, but only the mother seemed pleasant. Father and son were polite, but remote. I learned that Dad was a career military officer, Mom was a secretary, and the son was in the ninth grade.

"Let's get down to business and find out what's going on here," I said to get things started. "Let's see, Mother, I believe you called me to set this up. You said that you and your husband were concerned because John here has been lying, especially about his school grades. Does that sound like the problem?" I looked at the mother as I spoke.

"Yes," she answered, "John lies to both of us, and we felt we needed to talk with someone about this."

"How does that sound?" I turned to the father. "Does that sound pretty accurate to you?"

"Yes," he replied. "John's lying has increased markedly over the past year or so."

I asked specifically when he lied and to whom. I learned he lied to both parents, but only about his schoolwork. Whenever he

17

lied, his mother in particular became very angry with him, letting him know how bad he was and how disappointed she was in him.

We continued to talk. I found that the boy was far from being a disinterested son; in fact, he seemed to be quite a worrier. He worried a lot about his poor performance. But more than that, he worried about his parents' *responses* to his poor grades.

Probing further, I learned that the father had had a poor time in school. Moreover, his parents had never prodded him or expected him to do better, and he resented this. In his son he saw his own poor performance being lived out again. And he was convinced he should push his son the way he wished his parents had pushed him.

The mother had helped her son since he first entered school. Her assistance was crucial because the family had moved a lot. This cultivated a special closeness between mother and son. As they grew closer, the father felt more and more like an outcast. He withdrew, and the mother perceived this as a lack of caring. (At this point I could have chosen to explore the parents' marriage, which I sensed was strained. Following my custom, however, I did not, because they had not come to discuss their marriage. I respected this and continued with the task at hand. If at some later point they wished to talk about their marriage, I would be ready.)

Now the pattern was established. The father worried that his son would follow his academic path and so needed to be prodded. At the same time the father felt pushed to the periphery by the closeness between mother and son. The mother worried that she had not been able to tutor the son adequately in areas in which he needed special help, such as reading. My frame for the family dynamics was this: "When your son's report card comes out, it's not just his report card, it's the family report card." This in particular gave the teenager a "how could you do this to me?" message. Being sensitive, he decided to postpone the agony and hurt a little by lying to his parents about his grades.

I asked the boy if he thought his parents could cope if he were honest about a poor performance in school. He thought they could. I asked the father to take charge of the son's homework. From then on, the boy was to report on his homework to his father and to seek his father's help. I recommended this course of action for two reasons. First, this moved the father from a peripheral position with the boy to a close, working position while putting some distance between mother and son. Second, it created a different situation for everyone to see what would happen.

After only two weeks, the intervention apparently worked. The boy stopped lying; the level of tension in the family decreased. I warned the family that this could be only temporary. Because the boy was extremely protective of his parents, he might begin to shield them once again by lying if he detected that their disappointment was increasing. Follow-up several months later showed that the teenager was remaining honest.

Understanding family relationships requires a way of thinking that we are inclined not to use because we tend to pay attention to the wrong issues. This chapter examines the type of thinking that fosters a better understanding of relationships. Actually, understanding a relationship and understanding a metaphor are similar ways of thinking, using the same side of the brain. Therefore it is important to understand how the brain works as the groundwork for understanding how we perceive relationships.

## How the Brain Works

Although the human brain appears to be a single organ, it is in fact a double organ that consists of two identical-looking spheres joined together by a bridge of nerves called the *corpus callosum*. For a long time scientists believed that the left and right sides of the brain performed the same functions. In recent years, however, it was discovered otherwise.

The first revelation came when doctors began surgically to cut the corpus callosum in epileptic patients to try to stem the "electrical storms" the seizures generated. The doctors came to realize that they had cut the communication lines between the left and right sides of the brain. In experiments clinicians stimulated one side of the brain to see how it responded without interference from the other side.

The researchers discovered that each side of an adult's brain causes a fundamentally different way of thinking. Each side has its own way of knowing the world. The sides react differently to environmental stimuli and not always to the same stimuli. An attempt to "speak" to either side must be made in that side's "language" for the message to be received and processed.

We now know that in a child the right and left sides are much less differentiated than in an adult. They develop a working relationship something like a partnership. As a side is reinforced over time with a particular task, the other side will let the first side handle the chore.

Ideally each side does what it is best suited to do. When a problem develops, the side that is more competent to do so will take the lead in dealing with it; the other side contributes what it can to produce a complete and complementary answer. It is not possible to think consciously in both sides at once, but the conscious, thinking side can use the resources of the other side automatically. It has been found that people tend to favor one side over the other when solving problems.

In essence, each of us has two functioning minds that are ideally capable of working together to tackle the world outside and the world within ourselves. However, there is not as much communication *between* the sides as there is *within* each side. In critical situations, when conflict arises, the two "minds" may be unable to communicate with each other and instead may have conflict. (Note that the "left" and "right" brain characteristics are highly speculative among researchers, most of whom are comfortable with saying that the language function exists on the left side. But for the purposes of this book, "left brain" will serve as a convenient shorthand term for logical processes, while "right brain" includes functions that are intuitive processes.)

## How the Two Sides Know

The left side controls language, reason, logic, and science. It uses language as a way of knowing the world. In the process, information is received, broken down, analyzed into component parts, sorted into cubby holes, and named. Some have called this *directed thought,* because it follows the laws of linguistic logic (grammar, syntax, semantics).

The left side works objectively. It analyzes data one step at a time, deducing an answer after going through a series of logical sequences. In other words, it handles problem solving in a similar fashion as the computer.

The right side is the world of imagery, metaphor, and symbols. It reacts to sensory input in a direct, more reflexive fashion. Feelings, therefore, retain immediacy and power. The right side is interested in what it sees and hears for the thing itself, not for what it stands for. Each tree becomes a unique, unrepeatable experience.[1] This side likes to see things in their totality. This type of thought has been called "undirected thinking," the stuff of dreams, fantasies, and other experiences of our inner world. This kind of knowing we call "intuition," because we just "know" something is right, even if we can't trace through the steps with the left brain to say how we know it to be true.

The right side lacks direction, however, only when compared with the direct thinking of the left side. While the left side moves along sequentially in a linear mode, the right side cannot analyze long sequences. Instead it analyzes "in parallel," viewing the entire stimulus as a unit and coming up with the answer in one stroke. While the left side plods along logically formulating answers, the right side assimilates many fragments and makes sense of these. The right side can thus see a small, insignificant gesture and know instantly what behavioral response is appropriate.

Consider the sides from a developmental standpoint. As a young child grows, communication between the parents and the child changes. For instance, when a toddler gets too close to a fire, the parents simply remove him. As the child gets older he is slapped or scolded, demonstrating that the nonverbal (right) mode of communication is still preeminent. As the child grows even older, the nonverbal cues pale in significance and the child is instructed and ordered verbally (left). As he reaches adolescence, the parents use explanation and reason to guide his behavior, with the young person given more opportunities to make up his own mind as to what he will ultimately do. Maturity brings the progressive use of verbal (left) communication over nonverbal (right) communication.[2]

Let's look now at the way the sides use signs and symbols. The left side is the digital side where meaning is expressed in arbitrary, conventional signs (that is, a sign has no recognizable physical similarity to the object for which it stands). The best example of this is a word (the left side, of course, uses words in language). In regard to the word *cat*, we notice that there is no readily apparent connection between the word *cat* and the objective reality of the fuzzy animal who bears that name. Instead, societies come to agreement on what digital signs in language will represent which objects or relationships.

The right side uses a part of an action to signal something about the whole. This is analogical in that there is a likeness between the sign and the object represented. A good example of this is a photograph of a cat; the picture is a pretty good representation of the animal. The right side thinks in pictures, not in words. Other examples of right-brain symbols include maps, onomatopoeic words (e.g., hiss, bang), and allegories.

Perhaps another point should be made regarding the capacity of the right side to understand allegories, analogies, and metaphors. A metaphor is a figure of speech in which a word or phrase is used in place of another word or phrase to suggest a likeness between them. An analogy is a resemblance in some particulars between things otherwise unlike. The left brain cannot handle a metaphor or an analogy. These figures of speech, as they occur in communication, require the special skills of the right brain to "figure them out." Humans learn how to express feelings and thoughts using an image metaphor that the right side can construct easily (e.g., "I'm high as a kite today"). Sometimes our right brains concoct metaphors for us without our being consciously involved, as when we dream. Evidently when we dream, the left side doesn't participate much, and logic is therefore lacking in the images and stories we see.

Life must be a dynamic interplay between the left and right sides. Music, sports, and driving a car must be learned left-brained—in a sequential fashion. However, if we want to enjoy a symphony, the left side cannot help much. The right side hears the totality of the symphony and appreciates it as a unit. All sports and most habitual activity likewise are carried out by the right brain, which maps the activity and then carries it out quite effortlessly and unconsciously.

The right brain is basically "unconscious," for it accomplishes its business with little conscious attention. Much of its work is beyond awareness because of this automatic quality to it. If we were to break down into separate steps the myriad behaviors that we perform each day, we would never get anything done. Much of life needs to be carried out on "automatic pilot." One way to confuse unconscious tasks is to make them conscious. A good example of this is a golf swing. A skillful golf swing must be learned by the left brain, then incorporated into the right brain as an automatic sequence of behaviors. People who think about keeping arms straight, weight distributed, and grip proper during their swing will invariably hit the ball wrong. It has to unfold automatically.

The brain's right side is the one that understands and carries out relationships among people. The qualities that make relationships possible reside on the right side. The left side is also involved, but if it were the only negotiator, it would destroy relationships; it attends to the wrong things. It perceives relationships wrongly. People cannot be thought of as objects or as abstract principles. Relationship demands incarnation, and it is the right side that best understands this.

When people are seen relationally, all of human life must be thought of as an indivisible entity—that is, holistically. Human behavior is not sectioned off for separate, step-by-step analysis. Everything a person does has physical, social, psychological, and spiritual ramifications. Take as an example a person breaking his leg. This physical difficulty resonates through his mental, social, psychological, and spiritual life in various ways. It is impossible to have an event in a person's life isolated to one dimension.

Likewise, whatever affects one relationship of a person affects all that person's relationships, because problems permeate all of a person and consequently all his relationships. The whole person acts and relates and is defined by these relationships. People exist as whole entities unto themselves while they also exist as a part of larger wholes (organizations) to which they relate. The brain's right side responds as if it could see the whole individual with his unique characteristics while at the same time viewing his participation in larger groups (family, church, corporation, community).

Many people in the West, trained and conditioned to think in terms of "high technology," have difficulty with relational concepts. We trip over scriptural passages in which evil kings lead a whole nation into sin, in which fathers convert and the whole household follows suit, in which sins pass from generation to generation. We like to see the individual acting freely, unrestrained by outside influences. But when in fact the investigation of man is stretched beyond the analysis of the individual, the rich tapestry of contextual interactions becomes more vivid.

Accurate perception of the world demands balance between the brain's left and right sides. Unfortunately this is rarely achieved. Individuals and cultures perpetually emphasize one side over the other—one side is exalted, the other debased. Imbalance can skew the artist, the scientist, the theologian, the lover.

As Christians we find ourselves in a unique position. We are persons who are indwelt: Christ in us and we in Christ. This connection between Christ and humankind, however, is not the type of union that obliterates distinction. That is Eastern thought. For the Christian, union (right) must always involve distinction (left). However, we must also guard against a distinction that obscures union. This is the emphasis of the Greco-Roman gods and philosophies that contaminate Western thinking.

What follows is a partial list of the qualities attendant in the two sides.

| Left | Right |
|------|-------|
| Verbal | Spatial |
| Analysis | Synthesis |
| Intellectual | Intuitive |
| Deductive | Imaginative |
| Historical | Timeless |
| Explicit | Implicit |
| Directed | Free |
| Objective | Subjective |
| Vertical | Horizontal |
| Realistic | Impulsive |
| Rational | Metaphorical |
| Serial | Parallel |
| Abstract | Concrete |
| Digital | Analogical |
| Scholasticism | Mysticism |

Now that the concept of "sidedness" has been established, let's turn our thoughts to the implications of this phenomenon.

## What Is Reality?

How do we know what is really there? This has been an intriguing philosophical question since the dawn of time. As Christians we know that God created all that is, and he knows reality absolutely. All else is an approximation of what is really there.

This means that each of us has a unique perspective of real, but we must not confuse it with true reality. The best way to understand this is with a road map. The road map is not the actual terrain, but rather a representation of the terrain.

My map of reality is a compilation of all my opinions, assumptions, convictions, values, influences, and experiences. As I grow, my mind attempts to make sense of all it experiences—to interpret this and ascribe value and meaning to it.

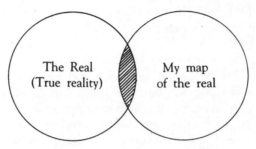

Figure 1.1. **Mapping Reality**

Most people, especially Christians, have difficulty distinguishing between the landscape of the mind and the landscape of actuality. Many Christians take great pains to explain their systems of truth, be it theology or Christian walk, but forget that what they say is the reality that is constructed in their heads, reflecting their unique perspective on the true reality. (Of course, the Holy Spirit comes into the life of the Christian and is therefore involved in altering the maps. But even with his assistance, our reality remains only an approximation of the true reality.) If humankind had never sinned, these two realities wouldn't have emerged; we would live in the true reality and know it all the time.

It would appear that the brain's right side synthesizes our experience of the world into an image, or map.[3] This makes sense in that the right side is the side that synthesizes and deals with wholes. The left side then has the task of rationalizing this map, separating the whole into subject and object and drawing the consequences.

People operate out of their internal maps.[4] As we encounter new experiences, we take out our map to give us the perspective on those events. In fact we are directed through all of life using our map to guide us. This map works much the same as the embedded commands that are part of a word-processing program. Embedded commands tell the printer how to react to certain sections of the text. The reader will never see these commands; they are used outside of awareness.

Most people are not aware that each of us has a map neatly tucked away within the right side of the brain. That map is rarely, if ever, taken out and analyzed. We don't see the map, we see *with* the map, all the time believing that the way we are perceiving the world and our unique experiences is what is real (first order as God knows it to be).

Interestingly, researchers feel the left side is committed to interpreting all of our overt behavior and emotional responses. Evidently this is done so that the brain can have a consistent theory of all that is happening at any given time. Sometimes the left side will go to bizarre lengths to correlate events. Unfortunately the theories the left side constructs frequently contradict the tenets of the maps on the right side, as we shall see in chapter 3.[5]

How does the map develop? A part of the map is contributed genetically (although the newborn infant, of course, has certain limitations physically and neurologically). There is also a part that is transmitted by the community, beginning with parents and family. As the person grows and develops, certain behaviors and experiences are permitted him while others are denied. Role assignments are learned. Various traits, talents, and abilities— quiet, athletic, outgoing, high-strung—as well as likes and dislikes emerge. The family continually guides this process, helping the child form his unique perspective on the world—his map.

The growing individual selects and interacts with others, building a social network in accordance with the internal map of expectations and options. Being unconscious and automatic, the map is not scrutinized by the developing individual. It is instead reinforced with the person's selective behavior and perceptions. During adolescence, the map is given its finishing touches as the varying, sometimes conflicting facets of the map are integrated and brought together into a working whole that provides, as David

Elkind states, "continuity with the past and focus and direction for the future."[6] It must always be remembered that the map is a dynamic entity, never a fixed and final component of a person.

The dynamic of the map is especially evident when the map is seen vis-à-vis relationships. The map is virtually held in place by interaction and has a self-fulfilling component to it as we consider how the map is used in relationships.[7] Suppose a person's map says that the world is a dangerous place to live in and people are not to be trusted. As the individual interacts with people, he will probably present himself as suspicious, hostile, sensitive to innuendo—the very characteristics that elicit from others responses that confirm his worst fears. This crystalizes that component of his map. Likewise, the happy, secure person perpetually evokes responses from people that confirm his map of the world as a safe, supportive place.

It is imperative that our map contain within it God's perspective on life and relationships as well as a wide range of options so that effective choices can be made in any given situation. In other words, we seek to have the two circles in figure 1.1 become more and more equal to each other.

## Summary

To help us think about relationships effectively, we must understand how each of us sees the world and fashions reality.

We experience and organize the world using two sides of our brains that carry out their work in fundamentally different ways. The left side of the brain breaks down data into component parts, labels them through language, and generally moves along in a step-by-step fashion.

The right side sees data holistically. It arrives at decisions instantaneously; it understands metaphors, noting resemblances between objects. It is the creative side where ideas spring into consciousness, seemingly from nowhere. It is also the side that understands and monitors relationships.

All of life must be a dynamic interplay between the sides. Unfortunately the left has gained ascendancy in the technological society, thus thrusting the right side's perspective to the background. This has caused a more "leftward" orientation in many areas of Christianity, where proposition (left side) takes precedence over worship (right side).

Reality for the believer springs from two sources: (1) the reality that is actually there because the Creator made it and sustains it, and (2) the "reality" that is fashioned in our minds and exists as a kind of map on the right side. In virtually any experience in life we take out our map to give us the proper reference for the experience and to guide our actions through the experience.

Both sides of the brain are critical in considering God and all he has made and considering man and his responsibilities before the Creator. When the perspective shifts to one side or the other, distortion of the total picture occurs. Because we speak of relationships in this text, the right side may appear to get more emphasis. But it is critical to keep the balance with the left side, or the distortion will permeate this book.

## Notes

[1] Virginia Owens, "Seeing Christianity in Red and Green as Well as Black and White," *Christianity Today* (2 September 1983): 38–40.

[2] Robin Skynner, *Systems of Family and Marital Psychotherapy* (New York: Brunner/Mazel, 1976), 87.

[3] Paul Watzlawick, *The Language of Change* (New York: Basic Books, 1978), 42.

[4] Stephen Lankton and Carol Lankton, *The Answer Within* (New York: Brunner/Mazel, 1983), 12.

[5] Michael Gazziniga, "The Social Brain," *Psychology Today* 19, no. 11 (November 1985): 33.

[6] David Elkind, *All Grown Up and No Place to Go* (Reading, Mass.: Addison-Wesley, 1984), 8.

[7] Paul Watzlawick, "Self-fulfilling Prophecies," in *The Invented Reality: How Do We Know What We Believe We Know?* ed. Paul Watzlawick (New York: Norton, 1984), 95.

# 2
# Observing

The previous chapter examined how our minds see the world and fashion reality. It also demonstrated how difficult thinking about relationships is for many of us. But clear thinking only starts the journey of understanding relationships thoroughly. To view relationships fully and to deal with problem situations in relationships effectively, we must also gather information correctly. How is this accomplished?

Certainly one must be a careful and shrewd observer of human behavior, especially if one wants to become a professional family counselor. An ability to perceive is a learned skill, and we all can learn to do it better. In fact, there is a vast amount of information available to our senses that frequently eludes us. We limit the amount of information that we perceive to a small fraction of what we could gather. Much of what we miss would help us understand relationships better.

Listening is a valuable tool for both counselors and laypeople to use in gathering data. It allows us to hear what a person's left brain has to say about a problem and what the person has deduced the problem to be. The right brain, however, is also communicating indispensable information that must be taken into account to help a situation change. Noticing the messages of both sides of the brain increases our observational abilities.

Of course, there is the danger of labeling and categorizing people as we collect more information. Our left brain loves to do this, but reducing people to diagnostic categories can be damaging. We must remember that even though certain behaviors, actions, symptoms, or habits fall into recognizable categories, the uniqueness of the individual stands in significance above these categories. Men and women are the unique creations of God. With this as a backdrop, then, let us look at actions that can increase our understanding of relationships.

## Actions That Give Us Information

Animals perform actions and little else. But people have massive brains with which they are able to internalize behavior through the complex processes of abstract thought such as language, philosophy, mathematics, and allegory. Even though much of the action with people is internal, there are still many very simple actions performed by people. These actions are inborn and genetic (e.g., sucking) and may be discovered by ourselves, absorbed from society, or taught formally. In fact, far from being free-flowing, human behavior is divided into a long series of separate acts that follow each other unconsciously and spontaneously (right side).[1] Let's consider several classes of actions that can enhance an understanding of relationships.

The first class is that of gestures. A gesture is any action that sends a visual signal to an onlooker. We are obviously so accustomed to gestures taking place constantly around us that generally we tend not to take particular notice of them. They are there merely as a punctuation to our existence. Desmond Morris, a student of human behavior, divides gestures into two types: incidental and primary.[2]

Incidental gestures are mechanical movements that involve personal actions such as cleaning, rubbing, wiping, coughing, yawning, and stretching. These gestures carry secondary messages to the observer. We can learn about a person by the way that he does these mechanical actions. If you are near someone while you are reading this page, set the book aside for a moment and observe that person—doing so in such a way that the person is not aware of being observed. Notice some incidental gestures. See if you can guess the person's mood. Then try to make some assumptions about the person's personality. Is that person outgoing? tentative? shy? sincere? flighty? Whether or not you are right is irrelevant. The point is that you can make these assumptions about a person merely by noting incidental gestures. Unfortunately, we make many judgments about people unconsciously (right side) with only this type of information.

Primary gestures, by contrast, involve deliberate signaling. The face and hands are the most important parts of the body that give these gestures. First consider the face. The more highly developed the species, the more elaborate the facial muscles. Humans have faces capable of myriad poses; in fact, the human face transmits the bulk of nonverbal signaling. The subtle changes that our faces make as we talk with someone constantly sends information to that other person. For example, just the eyebrow position alone can convey moods of dismay, anger, and joy.

We also use hands to convey small mood changes. We tend not to notice consciously when the hands punctuate verbal communication unless they move in pronounced ways. Put this book down again, turn on the television set, but leave the sound turned down. Watch the characters on the screen gesture to one another. Notice their faces and their hands. Watch how varied and subtle the movements and changes can be.

Yet another class of actions involves postural changes. We can focus on the ways that people who are in agreement assume particular postures in relation to one another. It is interesting to note that friends who are conversing unconsciously (right side) act in unison. First, they will adopt a similar posture. Then, if they are particularly friendly and share an attitude on the subject currently discussed, their actions will become almost identical to each other. This is a natural, unconscious display of companionship and rapport.[3]

Slow-motion filming of this phenomenon has shown that there is a "microsynchrony" of small movements, so sensitive that it is hard to see with the naked eye. These movements include tiny, momentary dips and nods of the head, tensing of fingers, stretching of lips, and jerks of the body that become matched for the two people with strong rapport. Evidently the right side of the brain unconsciously registers the movements of the other, matches these through similar movements, and registers the feeling of warmth to the person. One reason why mental patients *are* mental patients is that they are literally not in "sync" with the rest of the world. For whatever reason, they have not learned how to match behaviors this way, so that others perpetually perceive them as strange.

Desmond Morris, who spent much of his life observing people's habits, includes one more important class of actions. He calls this "nonverbal leakage." These are clues that give us away, revealing our true feelings and intentions without our knowledge. Our right brain has a way of exposing us, even when we try to hide our true selves. As two people talk, points of tension in conversation will trigger internal feelings.

The right brain will also betray us when we lie. When a person lies, there is usually a decrease in frequency of hand gesturing with an increase in hand-to-face contacts (e.g., hand over mouth, hand touching nose). A lying person will also increase the number of body shifts.[4]

We all know how we feel if our face reddens when we want to appear calm, or if we stutter or stammer when we wish to come across "in control." Our bodies many times "betray" us just when we hope to impress. Let's look a little more closely at the ways in which our bodies send messages automatically.

Our bodies have a unique wiring system. We've already discussed the control panel (brain) a bit. Now consider what happens to us when we come under stress and are aroused to action. Our bodies are equipped with a particular wiring circuit called the "automatic nervous system." This system has two parts: one readies us for action (systematic), and the other calms us when the action ceases (parasympathetic). Most of the time these two parts are balanced. During times of stress, however, the sympathetic part takes over: adrenalin pours into the blood as the heart begins to pump faster; blood circulates away from the skin and viscera to the muscles and brain (you have to think fast to decide whether you should fight or run); digestion slows; saliva production decreases; breathing speeds up and deepens; sweat production increases.

To the trained observer (when changes are less apparent) or to the untrained observer (when changes are pronounced), it is obvious that stress placed on a person will yield particular signals: rapid breathing, dry mouth, loss of skin color, sweating, shifting body movements. These can be significant changes to note while trying to understand relationships.

Besides the changes that occur when pressure is applied, the body will signal other emotional events. Consider the pupil of the eye, an area that we usually do not think about consciously. Light affects both pupil size and emotional changes. Pupil changes are unconsciously emitted and received. As an example, when people feel emotional excitement, their pupils dilate. One researcher showed pictures of babies to various people. He found that all women and married men had pupil dilation. Unmarried men, however, had pupil constriction. When pictures of nudes of the opposite sex were shown to people, both men and women experienced pupil dilation. One final experiment involved two identical photographs of a girl. In one photo, however, the pupils were enlarged. People shown the pictures said the pupil-enlarged girl was more attractive.[5]

Pupil enlargement and constriction constantly occur as we converse with people. We notice these slight changes unconsciously and alter our behavior toward the person as a result.

Several other areas of human action emit changes that we register unconsciously. One is the voice. People constantly adjust the tone, the tempo, and the amplitude as they speak. When these changes are dramatic, we notice them consciously. If the changes are more subtle, we receive them unconsciously (on the right side). Our unconscious also notices all incidental limb movement and changes in body posture.

Most of us are surprised to discover just how much action takes place in the body as we talk. James Lynch is a doctor who has spent years researching changes in heart rate and related factors as people talk with one another. He states that for too long we, like Descartes, have viewed the body as a machine that is isolated in its functioning. Lynch cites study after study that demonstrates how the organs of the body respond and change dramatically with something as seemingly innocuous as human dialogue. He is also quick to state that many people tend not to realize their internal conflicts, and the battle rages with such symptoms as hypertension and migraines.[6]

This might be a good time to turn the television set back on and again notice the subtle movements taking place between the characters. Later on, we will discuss how these actions have communication value—they "speak" very powerfully to us—and influence our behavior. As counselors we need to be aware of this fact and use it to understand and bring about change in our clients.

Now let us turn from observing individuals to observing the family and see how to gather pertinent information about that.

## Observing Families

We must not only become accurate observers of individuals, but also develop an awareness of groups of people, particularly families. As families organize and carry on their business—a subject treated later in this book—various behaviors begin to emerge that warrant noting. The first of these is communication patterns. Here are some points that professional counselors notice in family communication patterns:

> Who sits where?
> Who initiates conversation?
> Who withdraws?
> What is the ongoing stance of family members (e.g., blaming, distracting, computer-like, placating)?
> Who is ignored?
> Do members make their wishes known?
> Are differences between members noted by other members?
> How are disagreements handled?
> Is there a pattern of communication flow (e.g., Mother speaks after each member speaks)?
> Who interrupts?
> Who clarifies?

Counselors also look at family roles and ask questions that can clarify family functioning.

> Who supports whom?
> Who criticizes whom?
> Who is the family mediator?
> Who protects whom?
> Who is the scapegoat?
> Who is the decision maker?
> Who disciplines or carries out family rules?

Now consider some general structural observations to question:

> Is the level of responsibility given to the children appropriate for
> their ages?
> Do parents intrude into children's business? Vice versa?
> Do parents take on children's problems as their own (e.g., fight
> their children's fights)?
> Who seems really to be in charge in the family; that is, who
> makes things happen and controls the flow? (This is often
> subtle, and we can be confused as to who is the real "shaker
> and mover" in the family.)

Of course, all families have problems. Here are some questions to
ask regarding any problem that could foster resolution:

> When does the problem occur (time of day, week, month)?
> Who is there when it occurs?
> What leads up to the problem behavior (step-by-step)?
> Who responds to the behavior?
> How do they respond?
> How are things resolved and returned to normal?

## Observing Couples

Much of what has been said about observing families can also
apply to observing married couples as they organize and carry out
their business. Here are several new angles to enlarge our
perspective of the relationship:

> Who starts conversations?
> Who talks the most?
> Do they pay attention to each other?
> When tense issues come up, how does each person react?
> Do some issues get sidetracked? How?
> Do they appear to be on equal footing intellectually?
> Who seems the more upset and concerned?

## Content Vs. Process

You may have noticed that of all the items we have cited to
observe, none of them necessarily has anything to do with
content—the substantive issues and problems that people have,
such as depression, rebellion, and anxiety. Instead, we have

presented the phenomena occurring all around us all the time that are largely ignored. These are the processes—the series of actions, changes and functions—that help produce a particular result.

Our environment, the context of our existence, and the processes tend not to be noticed consciously (left side). However, our unconscious (right side) attends to these matters constantly and makes necessary adjustments as a result. Unfortunately, we usually remain totally unaware of the influence these processes have on us. We don't see how they shape virtually every relationship.

We're so busy listening and attending to the content of what is said to us that the processes escape. It is as if there is another dimension to our daily living, acted out but not generally open to our scrutiny. A proper perspective on relational problems must take these processes into account. It is the processes themselves that go awry in relationships.

When people go to counselors with problems, they will describe the problems as they see them. Although a client's aim is not to deceive, a counselor who listens strictly to the content of the problem gains only a small amount of useful information. Many problems arise out of the process of ongoing living and relating between people. People use their left sides to ascribe the cause of a particular problem to a particular antecedent. As we noted in the previous chapter, the left side is continually theorizing about all behavior, trying to make sense of it. However, this information is invariably limited in scope, possibly misguided in focus, or fundamentally unhelpful and misleading. The alert counselor is one who can hear the problem as stated while at the same time attending to the vast amount of data fed from the right side.

We also tend to focus on the content and have particular difficulty attending to the process when the content involves areas where we as observers or counselors are intense. If the topic is sexual compromise, for example, and we personally have unresolved conflicts in this matter, it becomes very hard to reflect on the process before us. If we have had problems with alcohol and we are conversing with a man who has a history of alcoholism, it will probably be difficult to see how he and his wife interact around the problem; instead the focus will be on the problem of drinking itself.

Several examples demonstrate the way the process unfolds:

*Example 1*

A minister in a church keeps a tight rein on the ruling board of elders. He speaks to them quite harshly and presides over the agenda meticulously. (Don't be concerned about the issues on the agenda; note the process.) He does this because he senses constant criticism from the elders and fears that if he slackens at all, they will seize total control, rendering him powerless. Of course, the elders criticize continually because they are constantly badgered. The process feeds itself, regardless of the content issue before the board. Often church fights and splits have little or nothing to do with doctrine. It is the process—the way church life is carried out, the way people behave toward each other—that is the real issue behind the struggles.

*Example 2*

A young, single mother of a toddler lives at home with her mother. Her mother tells her continually to care for her child. When she moves to care for the child, the mother criticizes how she cares for him. The young mother withdraws. Her mother again criticizes her for not caring for the child. (Again, disregard the disciplinary techniques; just note the process.)

*Example 3*

A new husband attempts to reach accord with his wife on various tough decisions. (There is no need to know which decisions; just mark the process.) When the discussion becomes heated, his wife withdraws—she says she can't think straight under that much pressure. He feels abandoned by her, which makes him come on even stronger. This causes her to withdraw more. No issues are ever settled. Both feel hopeless.

*Example 4*

A husband and wife, married five years, decide to have a baby. They try for years and nothing happens. They are unable to get on with their lives, to make career and educational decisions, where to live, and so on, because of the possibility of having a baby and having to alter their plans. As a consequence, their lives are stalled, and the issue of having a baby looms bigger and bigger in their minds until it is an obsession.

*Example 5*

A man marries a divorced woman who has two teenaged daughters. He feels threatened moving into an intact household where he is an outsider. But to gain respect he makes harsh demands on the girls about their behavior in and out of the house. They resent this and rebel, which only makes him feel less effective and causes him to be harsher still.

*Example 6*

A couple has a ten-year-old boy and a seven-year-old girl who fight mercilessly with each other, the boy coming within a hairsbreadth of really hurting his sister. It is discovered that the boy has no extra privileges for being older. He and his sister have been treated exactly the same all of his life—same bedtime, same curfew, and so on.

*Example 7*

A fourteen-year-old girl won't go to school. She has stayed at home for more than a month with vague complaints about being upset and afraid. Inquiries disclose that she is not afraid of anything in particular at school, and nothing unusual has happened to her there. Actually, when this first started, she really had been sick. When it was time for her to go back to school, she hesitated. Just when her parents needed to be definitive and firmly set the limits about her going back to school, they hesitated, concerned that she might have some "psychological problems." Their ambivalence fed her hesitation.

*Example 8*

A man in Africa has become the "head man" in his district. The "head man" post, which is like that of a judge, county executive, and chief all rolled into one, is hereditary, his father and grandfather having held the position before him. When this man, who is in his mid-forties, assumes the post, he is unsure whether he can fulfill the responsibilities. The older men in the village sense his tentativeness and voice their concern that he is too young. His ambivalence feeds their ambivalence even more. The symbol of his leadership is a pin that had been passed on to him by his father. Though he is to wear the pin at all times, he has never worn it, thus fueling the villagers' hesitation.

*Example 9*

A divorced older woman changes counselors after receiving counseling for some time following her divorce. She speaks with the new counselor for months about vague complaints (the content) that afflict her. The counselor is making no headway and finally realizes that his client has no motivation to change; if she changes she will lose the one thing she really needs—an uninterrupted chat once a week with a caring human being—the counselor—who takes what she has to say seriously.

*Example 10*

A sixteen-year-old boy is totally irresponsible. He will not manage his life, his time, or his money. He expects his father to bail him out of all difficulties. The father is a man who comes from a life of deprivation. Nothing was handed to him; he has had to scrape for everything he has. When he finally reaches success, he vows that his son will never have to suffer as he did. But the father doesn't realize that the whole process of suffering and deprivation is the force that motivated him and made him the responsible, farsighted achiever he is.

In the midst of this sea of information that can be gathered about people and their predicaments, what parts are important to bring about positive change? This is the central issue of both counseling and the understanding of how to improve our own personal relationships. If we all attended to all the content and all the processes that unfolded before us, we would be overwhelmed with data and would accomplish nothing. But gathering information about relationships requires particular care as well as attention to specific skills of observation.

## Summary

Both professional counseling and understanding personal relationships require gathering data, but which data? Often we ignore the processes of relationship in deference to the content expressed by the members of the relationships. But the information that the right side of our brain sends and receives about the ongoing processes of relationships needs special attention. These data are essential to understanding relationships.

This body of knowledge is largely ignored because it is usually not attended to consciously (on the left side). Consciously we listen to the words while the unconscious (right side) processes swirl around us. People reveal their internal state with a myriad of body signals. It becomes important to attend to these because more often than not, the person who talks about his problems is not completely aware of all the issues that comprise the problems. These signals can provide valuable clues.

As people come together and interact with each other in groups—family, church, community, business—the ways of inter- acting yield valuable information on what is wrong and how best to go about fixing it.

## Notes

[1] Albert Scheflen, *Body Language and the Social Order* (New York: Prentice-Hall, 1972), 26.

[2] Desmond Morris, *Manwatching* (New York: Abrams, 1977), 24.

[3] Ibid., 83–84.

[4] Allan Pease, "Signals," in *Readers' Digest* (December 1984): 135.

[5] Morris, *Manwatching,* 169ff.

[6] James J. Lynch, *The Language of the Heart* (New York: Basic Books, 1985), 6–7.

# 3

# Communicating

W e have so far considered how we perceive the world in different ways with the two sides of our brain. We have also discovered that understanding personal relationships for either counselors or laypeople requires good observation skills so that processes can be detected. Now we are going to consider how people communicate to others their observations and perceptions about the world.

Communication can be defined in various ways. The dictionary might define it as the exchange of messages or the acquisition and retention of information. Jurgen Ruesch and Gregory Bateson, communication theorists, cast a broader net when they define communication as all those processes by which people influence one another.[1] Virginia Satir, a family therapist, has a different twist when she speaks of it as all these symbols and clues used by people in giving and receiving meaning.[2] Of course we know that communication is the vehicle through which community and personhood are made possible.

## The Two Parts of Communication

There are no "simple messages" in personal communication. This is because we send more than one message every time we communicate.

When most people think of communicating or sending messages, they think that there is only one part to the message: the content of the message, that is, the actual words that are spoken. Because this is the conscious part of communication, it is logical to assume that most people would be aware only of this part. As you might suspect, the content comes from the left side of the speaker's brain and is processed on the left side of the hearer's brain.

But the content level is only one part of the message. The right side also participates in all communication, for that side catches the relational messages that are sent. The right side scans communication for other messages as the left side hears the content. The right side wants to know, What is the relationship between me and the speaker? How should I interpret the content of the message? The right side tunes in on the way the message is said.

Where does the right side search for these messages? Certainly not in the content; that's the territory of the left side. Instead, it looks at body language, tone of voice, facial expression, pupil dilation, and so on. Remember that in chapter 2 we talked about the multitude of messages sent as a person converses with us. Gesturing, body movement, pupil dilation all give us information that has nothing to do with content. Now we see that these motions have tremendous communication value, for this is the speaker's right side communicating to the listener's right side about their relationship.

Why do we say that the right side communicates the relationship messages through nonverbal means? The right side contains our map, our game plan for living. It contains our real feelings about ourselves and others and how we see ourselves in the context of other people. This side does not have language at its disposal. It communicates the best way it can with what is available—nonverbal things such as posture, facial expression, and tone of voice. As this side communicates over a long period of time, it does so through habitual actions and lifestyles.

When a person sends a message to another person, obviously the speaker has a particular intent. The speaker knows how he wants the listener to respond to the message. However, the impact of that message on the listener may be totally different from what the speaker intended. For instance, a wife says to a husband, "Close the door." This is a seemingly innocuous message. She may be dumbfounded to find herself in a bitter fight with her husband simply because the intent of her message—to have him close the door—affected him negatively.

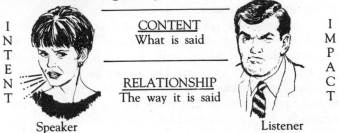

| | | |
|---|---|---|
| I N T E N T | CONTENT<br>What is said<br>——————<br>RELATIONSHIP<br>The way it is said | I M P A C T |
| Speaker | | Listener |

Figure 3.1

The goal of communication is to have the intent equal the impact. However, this is not achieved much of the time, especially in close interpersonal relationships. When the impact on our listeners does not correspond to what we intended for them to hear, wild arguments may ensue—especially if we are conversing with our spouse.

"You never listen to me!"

"I'm speaking to you in plain English. Are you dumb or something?"

Richard Bandler and John Grinder write that the meaning of our communication is the response we get, period.[3] There is no sense in arguing what we meant by a particular statement; the impact on the hearer is all that matters.

## Relational Messages

The right side sends and receives the relational messages. Remember, these messages are not sent verbally and are probably out of the awareness of the speaker and listener. But they elicit strong responses from the listener.

The first message says, "I'm in charge (or control or command) of you (this situation or our relationship)." We may call this a "one-up" message because the speaker appears to be communicating that he is "up" or in a position of apparent strength.

The other message says, "I'm not in charge (command or

control) of you (this situation or our relationship). I'm beneath
you." We may call this a "one-down" message because it is the
position of apparent weakness.

These messages are sent and received and reacted to on an
unconscious level. Unfortunately, we tend to believe that a person
who is communicating one-up really is in charge of the situation,
when in the majority of cases the opposite is true. Take for
instance the loud, brassy, bossy individual whose messages are
communicated nonverbally. Often these people feel they are never
taken seriously; hence they tend to come on strong. They present
their relational message as one-up.

The apostle John speaks of this in the book of Revelation
when he writes to the church at Laodicea:

> You say, "I am rich; I have acquired wealth and do not need a
> thing." [An obvious one-up message.] But you do not realize that
> you are wretched, pitiful, poor, blind and naked (Rev. 3:17).

If we react to the one-up person as though he is really in
charge, we run into all kinds of difficulties, because underneath
that person (right side) experiences himself as weak. Let's take as
an example the wife-beater. The person who bullies his wife to
keep her in line has to be the epitome of one-upmanship. Most
social agencies attack the abuser as though he were in fact in
charge of the situation. Salvador Minuchin, a family theorist,
borrows a concept from an Israeli sociologist to point out that there
are in fact two kinds of violence: *Coercive*, in which the action is
controlled and purposeful, and *pleading*, in which the offender feels
that he himself is a victim. Wife-beaters fall into the latter
category, thinking of themselves as helpless responders. In fact,
many see themselves as inferior in every way to their wives.
Violence is the only means they can recognize to achieve any kind
of parity.[4]

Heeding these relational messages is critical to understanding
why people react to each other the way they do. Sometimes the
messages can take on comical proportions. One exchange found
commonly among Christian couples is the wife who demands that
her husband be the head of the house. This is a hopeless paradox,
for the wife takes a one-up demanding stance and insists her
husband be one-up. He is put in a bind, for he must either yield to

his wife (go one-down) and try to take the lead, or he must maintain some semblance of authority over her by denying her request and remaining a "wimp."

In Matthew 20, Mrs. Zebedee attempted to get Jesus to make her boys one-up with special places in the coming kingdom. Jesus responded that this one-up position is the way the world does things. If we want to be truly one-up (great in the kingdom), we must become the servant of all (one-down). The Christian message seems to move best from a one-down position.

> For the foolishness of God [one-down] is wiser than man's wisdom, and the weakness of God is stronger than man's strength. Brothers, think of what you were when you were called. Not many of you were wise by human standards [one-up]; not many were influential; not many were of noble birth. But God chose the foolish things of the world to shame the wise; God chose the weak things . . . the lowly things . . . the things that are not—to nullify the things that are, so that no one may boast before him (1 Cor. 1:25–29).

Scripture elegantly points out how these two positions work together. What *appears* to be strong, wise, noble (one-up) isn't. What *appears* to be one-down isn't.

Satan's initial temptation of Eve in the Garden captured this very point. He said to her, "You shall not die [the ultimate one-down position], but you shall be as God [the ultimate one-up position]."

## Congruent Messages

Both sides of our brain send and receive messages, and both sets of messages must be considered. It is absolutely critical that the messages coming from the left side (content) match the messages coming from the right (relationship). When they do, we say that a person is congruent. That sounds easy enough. We would think that most messages we send and receive are congruent. But this is not the case. Many times our content messages do not equal our relationship messages, and we are said to be incongruent.

An interesting experiment was conducted by Roger Sperry, who has worked extensively with people who have had brain surgery to control epilepsy (split-brain people). After this surgery, the left side of the brain can no longer converse and compare notes with the right side. Experiments can then be run to show how the two sides work.

In one experiment, Sperry showed the right side a color—only the left eye was open. The verbal left side could not see the color and attach the correct name to it. He then asked the persons to guess which color was flashed. As the left side made incorrect guesses, the right side communicated its disapproval by the only means available to it, through frowns and headshakes.

In this manner we send incongruent messages. The verbal message says one thing, our nonverbal messages another: "I am *not* angry!" the person screams with a furrowed brow and threatening stance. What happens when we send an incongruent message? There are several things the listener can do. He can accept the verbal and ignore the nonverbal, relational message. He can do the reverse, accepting the nonverbal. Or he can point up the discrepancy: "Gee, you said you weren't angry, but did you notice how loud and threatening you were when you said that?"

Most people are not communication experts and would not have the presence of mind in a heated exchange to point up an incongruency. So what do most people do when faced with an incongruency? They reject the content and accept the relational message. This makes sense if in fact the relational message comes from the part of us that contains our game plan of life. Scripture is loaded with references to the need for congruent messages and the problems that arise from incongruent messages:

> If I speak in the tongues of men and of angels [content], but have not love [relational], I am only a resounding gong or a clanging cymbal (1 Cor. 13:1).

> What good is it, my brothers, if a man claims to have faith but has no deeds? Can such faith save him? Suppose a brother or sister is without clothes and daily food. If one of you says to him, "Go, I wish you well; keep warm and well fed," but does nothing about his physical needs, what good is it? (James 2:14–16).

> We know that we have come to know him if we obey his commands. The man who says, "I know him," but does not do what he commands is a liar, and the truth is not in him. But if anyone obeys his word, God's love is truly made complete in him. This is

how we know we are in him: Whoever claims to live in him must walk as Jesus did (1 John 2:3–6).

These are powerful passages. They let us know that we can manipulate propositional truth, know it and verbalize it, and still be incomplete in our spiritual expression. The biblical message is not just propositions that are believed; it is a life that is walked. True conversion is congruent change. There is a chorus that speaks to this incongruity in Christian faith.

> What you are speaks so loud,
> That the world can't hear what you say.
> They're looking at your walk,
> Not listening to your talk.

Our relational messages come from the right side where our map is. We rarely take that map out to check it, consider what is there, and make needed corrections. Because of this, many times we don't even realize how powerful our relational messages are. We don't realize that we say one thing and do another.

Many people in the church lie "wounded and bleeding" because of incongruent messages. We tell people that in God's eyes we are all alike, but in practice we elevate certain people over others because of their social standing (James 2:1–4), their sex, spiritual gifts, or race. We say we are equally guilty before a holy God and that sin is not ranked in his eyes. Yet we are repulsed by the deeds some have previously committed.

### Further Complications in Communication

We have seen how in communication the left side contributes the "what" of the message, the right side adding the "way." Moreover, the right side communicates with words along with the body language. But the words are used differently from the left side.

As we have said, all persons have a map on their right side that guides their behavior. People need a rich map in which they can perceive a wide, biblical range of options when crises and transitions—marriage, death, job transfer—arise.

When people speak of their experiences, they draw from their map and represent that data in words, that is, linguistically. At this point the nonverbal right side goes to the left side to get the proper words to express what needs to be said. It is here that problems arise, for although language is a great gift from God for communication, it also has a number of danger points that must be considered.

Remember, language is a symbol system used on the left side. Therefore, when we hear and use language, the tendency is to use it in a precise, logical way in which each statement has a single and specific referent—when we talk about a chair, we mean a chair. Using language in this way, the words chosen are basically nouns—persons, places, and things. This is the way language is used when we deal in science or theology or other left-side business. Sharp, precise distinctions are made between objects; time and movement are frozen.

Unfortunately, we tend to think that this precise use of language is also in effect when we talk to each other about experience, which always involves relationship. But experience has to do with motion, and the words used are verbs. Verbs lead us into journeys through time. No longer are we static; we are dynamic. We can only express relational experiences by using action: "He *did* this," not, "He *is* this." People tend to represent ongoing processes (verbs) as fixed events (nouns), and in so doing they lose both control of and the ability to influence those events.[5]

Our personal experience begins to lead us into the right side of the brain. This is, of course, the area where moving pictures dominate. But not only is there movement in relationships, there are also nouns and concrete ideas. Nouns and the stuff of concrete ideas, however, are used differently in this region; because metaphor and analogue hold sway, messages have multiple referents. When language is used metaphorically, each message refers to a context of other messages—as in play, ritual, and art.

Analogue places us in the realm of story. Stories have a way of circumventing the left, logical side of our mind and accessing the right side, where the map is kept. A "righteous man" asked Jesus, "Who is my neighbor?" (Luke 10:29). This is a good philosophical question that demands a rational answer. Instead of listing several propositions about neighbors to this man, however, Jesus told a story about a man on a journey who is mugged by thieves, then rescued by a Samaritan.

Notice in this story the two elements of the right side: the movement of relationship and the use of metaphor. The reverses in this story leave the original questioner totally defenseless against the implications of neighborliness.

Multiple metaphoric messages are sent whenever people communicate. We tend to send messages metaphorically when it is difficult for us to say them directly. They are out of our awareness and tucked neatly within the unconscious, right side. Conflict between two people is often channeled metaphorically, resulting in the submersion of the conflict. Thus the right brain of one person speaks with the right brain of the listener by way of metaphor. The left brain hears the words, but the right brain understands what is really being said. In a real way, as language passes between people, we resonate to and understand what is said on all levels of our experience, the left side extracting certain points to note, the right side extracting others. Because the left brain is the "conscious" side, we tend not to realize that connections are also being made in the right.

To illustrate this point, let's take the case of a mother who took her nineteen-year-old daughter to a counselor. The girl was depressed and passive. She also complained of a pain in her neck. As the three talked about the girl's difficulties, the counselor noted how intrusive the mother was in the girl's life. It became obvious that the mother was, quite literally, a pain in the neck! The girl could not express this directly to her mother, so her right side had designed this ingenious symptom to signal the difficulty.

If the right brain uses metaphor to make itself known, then the world of stories, jokes, myth, and figurative language would be the proper way to communicate with this side of the brain. Counseling in general—and Christian counseling in particular—has attempted to change behavior by appealing to the left side of the brain. By this method, propositional truth is given to a person in an attempt to enlighten him as to his difficulty (insight) and thus bring about change. The idea is that if a person knows why he does or does not do something, he will immediately alter it. This approach, not incidentally, has been most effective for many problems.

However, the map exists on the other side of the brain, the side that is not responsive to logical suggestions. One theorist states that this side of the brain needs its own language to make changes.[6] Logical, propositional explanations do not penetrate to this side. Jesus clearly seemed to understand this point in his use of parables. Gordon Fee and Douglas Stuart discuss the function of a parable as being similar to a joke. To interpret a parable—that is, to use the left side—is in some ways to destroy it. The parable bypasses the logical left side and calls for an immediate response from the right side. It "catches" the listener as the punchline is delivered. There is no room for analytical discourse; the point is lodged within the right side before this can occur.[7]

This suggests that counseling that involves the right side would need to include stories, possibly jokes, the use of inner healing (guided imagery that has the person see himself in various troubling situations, but with Christ present to dispel the emotional responses), and the rearrangement of relationships. Of course, counseling is not an either-or proposition. In dealing with hurting people, various situations call for the use of many interventions that obviously involve both sides of the brain.

## Summary

God gave us the gift of communication whereby he could construct and maintain his relationship with us (on the vertical plane), and likewise we with others (on the horizontal plane). It is virtually impossible to imagine God acting in his creation without communication, because all of relationship presupposes it.

Like all God's gifts, communication must be understood and handled with care, for the consequences of improper use are far-reaching.

Both sides of our brains give and receive messages. The left side works with words and uses these to send messages. The right side uses body language and some words used metaphorically to get across its meaning. It is hoped that as we give our messages to others, the right-side and left-side messages will be congruent, in harmony. If they are not and what someone says doesn't equal the way he says it, confusion will result in the mind of the hearer.

We must be in tune with what people say and the way they say it. But even more than this, we must realize that as we speak, we are to a degree limited by the words we choose. In using certain words to express how we feel and in listening to the words of others, the danger lingers that the meaning behind the words will be misunderstood.

# Notes

[1] Jurgen Ruesch and Gregory Bateson, *Communication: The Social Matrix of Society* (New York: Norton, 1951), 37.

[2] Virginia Satir, *Conjoint Family Therapy* (Palo Alto, Calif.: Science and Behavior, 1967), 63.

[3] Richard Bandler and John Grinder, *Reframing* (Moab, Utah: Real People, 1982), 34.

[4] Salvador Minuchin, "A Day in Court," *Family Networker* 8, no. 6 (November-December 1984): 40.

[5] Richard Bandler and John Grinder, *The Structure of Magic, I* (Palo Alto, Calif.: Science and Behavior, 1975).

[6] Paul Watzlawick, *The Language of Change* (New York: Basic Books, 1978), 48ff.

[7] Gordon Fee and Douglas Stuart, *How to Read the Bible for All Its Worth* (Grand Rapids: Zondervan, 1982), 126.

# 4
# Changing

An overriding theme of the Bible is the need for change in relationship. One crucial aspect of God's making humankind in his image is our ability to enter into relationships. The Fall severed the vertical relationship between God and mankind. This relationship needs restoration before any horizontal relationship can move toward complete healing. Without the healing of the primary, vertical relationship, all other relationships are contaminated.

Scripture focuses extensively on the restoration of all these relationships. Two illustrative verses:

> Therefore, if anyone is in Christ, he is a new creation (2 Cor. 5:17).

> May God himself, the God of peace, sanctify you through and through. May your whole spirit, soul and body be kept blameless at the coming of our Lord Jesus Christ (1 Thess. 5:23).

Christians are people who expect change. And they expect change to occur dramatically. They have seen this happen for themselves and others. The word *conversion* captures the essence of the change. Conversion involves a turning around, a transformation. Joseph Alleine, a New England Puritan, put it this way:

> Conversion is not the putting in a patch of holiness; but with the true convert holiness is woven into all his powers, principles, and practice. The sincere Christian is quite a new fabric, from the foundation to the topstone. He is a new man, a new creature.[1]

52

Jonathan Edwards also described this change.

> Those gracious influences which are the effects of the Spirit of God
> are altogether supernatural—are quite different from anything that
> unregenerate men experience. They are what no improvements, or
> composition of natural qualifications or principles will ever produce;
> because they not only differ from what is natural, and from
> everything that natural men experience in degree and circumstances
> but also in kind, and are of a nature far more excellent. From hence
> it follows that in gracious affections there are (also) new perceptions
> and sensations entirely different in their nature and kind from
> anything experienced by the (same) saints before they were
> sanctified.[2]

A good place to begin to look at this change, then, is in the
matter of perspective. In justification God's perspective on the
person changes: he was a sinner, now he is a saint. In sanctification
the believer's perspective begins to change. Now the person begins
to see life through God's eyes. Where does this perspective on life
reside? Though there is no simple answer to this, we can say our
perspective resides in a balance between what we hold to be true
propositionally (left side) and our map of reality that guides our
behavior (right side).

A striking example of change in perspective occurred in the
life of Elisha's servant. The king of Syria was furious with the
prophet Elisha and sent an army to surround the city and capture
him. The noise awakened Elisha's servant, who then looked out
the window and saw the city surrounded. Elisha attempted to calm
his servant down; then he prayed:

> "O LORD, open his eyes so he may see." Then the LORD opened the
> servant's eyes, and he looked and saw the hills full of horses and
> chariots of fire all around Elisha (2 Kings 6:17).

The servant's perspective was changed immediately. No longer did
he see a single man surrounded by a hostile army. He saw that
Elisha in fact had the upper hand. This change in perspective was
more than just a propositional understanding for the servant,
though that was surely part of it. His whole experience of the
situation was radically altered. He was no longer afraid of being
overrun by superior forces; he realized he was on the stronger side.
For us, this same type of change involves a radical reorientation of

our outlook on life, including our habits, thoughts, and values—
the way we respond to virtually any and every given situation.

Sanctification definitely has a strong propositional base. We
must know propositionally what we believe. This involves a
renewing of the mind to see what God has said about himself, life,
salvation, and so on. In this sense the propositional base is like the
superstructure of the building. But the picture is still incomplete.
Our propositions must change, and the maps that guide our
experiences must also change.

The map, we may recall, contains our perspectives on the
various experiences of life. The propositional superstructure sets
the limits of the map. This map unconsciously governs our actions.
We repeatedly take out our map to give us the "correct"
perspective on any given experience. If we are laid off from a job
because of production cutbacks, our map might label (or "frame," a
word we will use later) this experience as one more example of all
the bad luck that has befallen us all our "miserable life." If you are
a single male who notices a woman look at you and then look away
quickly, your map might label this experience as another female
rejection.

As the map begins to change, we begin to change our stance
in the various relationships of life, beginning at home. We are
obviously detailing a "domino effect." That, of course, is the
nature of relationship.

Professional counselors are involved in changing people.
When those people are Christians, the counselors actually become
instruments in the ongoing work of sanctification already in process
in those persons' lives.

## The Nature of Change

Two kinds of change will take place: the first-order change
and the second-order change.[3] First-order change involves minor
fluctuations of behavior within the bounds previously set. But it is
the second-order change that is at issue here: changing the
boundaries themselves.

An example of first-order change is changing the color of a
dress to be worn; second-order change is switching from a dress to a
pants suit. Pressing down on the gas pedal to change the speed of a
car is first-order; shifting gears is second-order. When Peter asked

Jesus how many times he had to forgive, Jesus offered a second-order change; he changed the boundaries of what would at that time have been considered acceptable: not seven times, but seventy times seven. This kind of action, of course, changes our whole relationship toward the one who wronged us.

First-order change appears logical, basically because it is a left-brain undertaking. So as problems arise, the solutions that follow are logical, even if they are not workable. If a person is defiant and won't do something, make him do it with force. If a baby cries all night, hold him and cuddle him. If a girl eats too much, tell her so every time you see her eating. If a person is afraid of a situation, avoid it.

Many hurting people are given first-order solutions to problems that require second-order change. Most commonsense solutions to problems are first-order, such as cheering up a depressed person.

Consider some case situations. A successful businessman and his wife sought counseling. From the outset of their marriage the wife would complain that she was inadequate, no good, and ugly—even though she was actually smart, pretty, and suitably employed.

Whenever she would launch into her litany of inadequacies, he would immediately begin to give reasons why she was adequate, pretty, and productive. This was a first-order solution. The husband would attempt to increase her confidence. But in building her up this way, his relationship with her always remained the same, that is, he was the parent ("one-up") caring for his inadequate child ("one-down"). The situation required a second-order change—for her to experience herself as his equal, instead of as his child. One way to accomplish this would have been for the husband to tell his wife each night what his inadequacies were and have her help him with these.

Another couple sought help because they were suffering sexual difficulties. Basically, she didn't want him to touch her at all. He would demand, then plead, to no avail. The problem with his pursuit of the issue was that he always came at her from the one-up position of strength, where he appeared powerful and she appeared problem-laden—frigid. The counselor struggled with the couple to try to help them overcome their problems, but he was unsuccessful.

Then the husband lost his job. When that happened, he lost his self-esteem and became depressed. Now he was obviously one-down and hurting badly. When his wife saw this, her sexual difficulties amazingly vanished; they no longer had sexual problems in their marriage.

In another case, a teacher in a second-grade classroom had a student who was totally unruly. The teacher punished him, threatened him, had the principal come and punish him, and held endless parent conferences, but still she failed to achieve the desired result. Then one day she put the problem boy in charge of maintaining discipline in the class; she never had another problem with him.

As you can see, second-order change involves changing the rules of the game, altering the perspective on a situation, and resetting the boundaries of the relationship. One author said it is "transforming one's way of experiencing the world."⁴ This definition sounds extraordinarily similar to the definition of conversion. In a biblical sense, conversion is a second-order change par excellence, for in this change God radically remakes the sinner into the saint, transforming his understanding (propositions) and his experience (maps).

In discussing the nature of relationships and how we can help to change them, we will necessarily be in the arena of second-order change. It is there that a Christian counselor in particular must be sensitive to the nature and direction of the changes he evokes.

Conversion is a vertical second-order change. The relationship between creature and Creator is altered. The Creator is the initiator and effector of this change.

Then we concentrate on the horizontal plane, where relationships exist between husband and wife, parent and child, child and child, employer and employee, and so on. In second-order change we work with the process more than the content. The goal is nothing less than a radical shift in the way a situation is perceived and experienced. For instance, Jesus commands us to "love your enemies." This means our whole perspective on our enemies has to change, for now they are to be objects of our love.

In first-order change, individuals, rather than relationships, are seen as the "site" of the difficulty. Though this is not a bad approach, it is often inadequate to produce desired changes.

Second-order change targets the processes of ongoing relationships, the right side that keeps maps. Obviously, if we are changing a map, we are changing the unconscious guidelines to behavior. Sanctification must be a second-order affair, where the very boundaries of existence are altered: "No longer I, but Christ. . . ." Again, understand that second-order change does include a strong propositional (left-side) component. But this type of change is a "domino" kind: the maps of perspective change, and this in turn changes our propositions, our habits, and our emotional responses.

Second-order change can be set in motion by a propositional shift: I once believed this, now I believe that. If change begins propositionally, it must carry through to the maps and alter the relationship for it to be a true second-order change: "Why do you call me Lord, and do not the things that I say?" Ideas (space) can be changed yet apparently have no effect in changing action (time) and ongoing experience.

Consider again the story about Elisha and his servant, for it has all the elements of a second-order change. When the Syrian army threatened, Elisha could have sat the servant down and gone over with him the facts of God's sovereignty, how God rules in the universe he created and how there is really nothing to fear. But there is a good chance the servant already knew this (left side). When he had the vision, everything fit together immediately. The truth mated with the experience, producing the emotional backup.

Christ's teachings are a virtual potpourri of second-order solutions that are seemingly ineffective:

"To be great in the kingdom, be the servant of all."

"God chose the foolish things to confound the wise."

"Love your enemies."

"Suffer the children to come, for of such is the kingdom."

It is logical that Jesus would seek to bring about second-order change, to change the maps that guide our behavior, to reorder all our relationships.

Theorists who have struggled with family relationships talk about second-order change in this way:

The occurrence of second-order change is ordinarily viewed as something uncontrollable, even incomprehensible, a quantum jump, a sudden illumination which unpredictably comes at the end of long, often frustrating mental and emotional labor—sometimes in a dream, sometimes almost as an act of grace in the theological sense.[5]

Second-order change is something that comes from outside the system (as opposed to first-order change which arises from within) and as a result is experienced by people as something quite unfamiliar and incomprehensible.

When first-order change is applied where second-order change is needed, difficulties arise. One team of therapists has shown how first-order solutions can lead to a perpetuation of the problem rather than to change.[6] For instance, there is the defiant teenager. Almost everyone who has had a teenager knows what defiance is all about. One first-order solution to such defiance is for the parents to demand respect. However, when anyone demands something of a defiant person, the results are almost always just more defiance.

So far we have spoken of second-order change in vertical and horizontal relationships. But the concepts are basically jumbled together. It is important to break down the concept of change and see how it operates practically in the lives of those who want to understand and strengthen relationships.

## The Practicality of Change

When people go to a counselor for help, they usually have a particular matter in mind that they want changed. Perhaps they want to be free of depression or they want their daughter to do better in school or they want their spouse to listen to them. Their idea as to what they want changed is usually very narrow and focused: "Change this symptom here," or "Change this member of the family."

Often these persons have already failed in their attempted first-order changes of themselves or their family members. Yet they expect the counselor to pursue change with more first-order plans. For example, a mother and father take a fifteen-year-old boy for counseling because he refuses to go to school. The parents' fruitless solution has been to yell at him. They present him to the counselor, anticipating that the counselor will now yell at him also.

The person who expects first-order change in effect says to the counselor, "Please change this person in this aspect. Leave the other aspects of him alone, and leave the rest of us alone, too. Thank you." People don't do this to be malicious; indeed, they don't even know they do it. But people do have an unconscious sense of how change should take place and to what extent. We all fear extensive changes—changes that involve the map—because our emotional security is bound up with the intactness of the map. We have seen it carefully constructed over the years. We will not yield easily to its being altered.

This is why counselors experience so much of what they call "resistance." They are dumbfounded to have people ask for help in changing and then fight the counselor every step of the way in the process.

But resistance can be a positive sign. When people resist change, counselors must respect them for two critical reasons. First, genuine lasting change is always tough, and to think about radical change is very threatening. Even though problem situations are debilitating, they are familiar for the person or family who has lived with a situation for a long time. Second, the people who seek help are demoralized because by going to a counselor they are already admitting defeat—that is, they have failed to solve a crucial problem. A part of them is invested in the counselor's failing, too, for if the counselor fails, the clients won't look so bad: "See, he couldn't bring change either."

## The Scope of Change

People go to counselors with problems and expect the professional to help them to change. But how much of the change process does a counselor effect? If the counselor is a Christian, does he seek their salvation immediately? Does he work to present them "complete in Christ"? And whom does he change? Does he work only with the individual? Or does he also work with the family? What about their community?

Much of the time there is a difference between what the person wants changed and what the counselor thinks ought to be changed. One striking example of this is the event of a non-

Christian seeking help from a Christian counselor. In the majority
of cases the person expresses no desire to become a Christian as
part of the change process. He is experiencing particular symptoms
that he wants relieved, period.

This leads us into the ethical issues of influencing people who
desire counseling. The old dichotomy was set up between the
directive counselors—who exerted a great deal of influence—and
the nondirective counselors—who exerted relatively little
influence. In the previous chapter we talked about the subtleties of
communication, how relational messages are communicated unconsciously, but powerfully. It is naïve to think, therefore, that
any counselor is nondirective and not influential in a client's life.
It is logical to assume that *all* counselors exert a very powerful
influence on their clients, whether they acknowledge this or not.
How he feels about a client, what he thinks is best in a given
situation, and in what direction he feels change should go are all
communicated to the people he counsels.

It is unwise to assume that a counselor can keep his values and
opinions out of a counseling situation. Certainly he can guard
carefully what he says at any given time. But the content is the
least powerful communication. Therefore it is helpful for a
counselor to be candid about his values. Numerous surveys have
shown that people go to those counselors who share their values.
However, we must realize that sometimes what a person says he
values and what he actually values are not the same.

Suppose, for example, a woman went to a counselor and asked
if he accepted women as equal to men. If that is one of his
conscious values, he would answer yes. However, as the counseling
unfolded, if his map contained many ambivalences about women
and his relationships with them, these ambivalences would begin
to surface—probably in nonverbal ways. Perhaps he would cut her
off when she expressed a meaningful opinion. Her right side would
pick up messages from his right side by the way he ordered his
relationship with her.

Counselors must try to maintain their focus. There are many
possible avenues to pursue, many pieces of information that can be
gathered. Out of all the data that are there, which are the most
important? And with these data, what distinctions should coun-

selors draw from them? How should they use them to bring about change?

Keep in mind that those who counsel also have maps on their right sides with which they get their perspectives on the people they seek to help. With the maps they hear problems and make particular distinctions on what is being said to them and how they will frame problems. They often set the stage for helping outside their own awareness that they are doing so.

The Christian counselor realizes that there are vertical as well as horizontal relationship considerations. For everyone who goes to him, there is the spiritual need present, either for justification (to get the spiritual life operating) or for sanctification (to continue the person's development toward Christlikeness). Justification involves purely vertical relationship aspects, while sanctification has both vertical and horizontal relationship aspects to it (loving the Lord and your neighbor). Whether or not a counselor focuses on these two issues, they are still there and will need attention at some point by someone.

Deciding which changes to attempt to initiate is admittedly not easy. Christian counselors are divided on this issue. Working in one area of relationship always has ramifications in the other relationships.

Consider also the manner in which counselors work. Some are comfortable working only with individuals. Others prefer couples and families. The latter believe that with a couple they will be more successful working with both partners and that by working with all members of a family they are less likely to miss vital information that could help them bring about change. If a counselor talks only to a teenaged boy about his life situation and never sees him in context interacting with his parents and siblings, he will have missed a great deal.

However, when the counselor is able to set in motion second-order change, many things can begin to change immediately. Once the rules of ongoing relationship have been altered, change begins to occur in a "falling dominoes" fashion. On this basis, a second-order change cannot occur in a person's spiritual life without also affecting mental, physical, and relational arenas. Concentration on and change in a person's psychological functioning will alter all other areas also. Not every aspect of a person's life needs direct attention from the counselor for change to occur there. The very nature of second-order change assures that this will happen.

One experienced counselor said that even though he has been counseling for many years, he is still continually humbled by the power and direction of change. Change occurs quite subtly for some people, but for others it swoops in like a mighty storm.

Counselors frequently ask themselves what their role should be in the change process. Sometimes they have to learn to step aside and allow change to take place in spite of them. Basically the counselor's role is to try to get the ball rolling in the right direction, to get the first domino to begin falling.

When I first went into counseling I thought that I had the tools to effect radical, "top-to-bottom" change and that it was my sworn duty to change everyone who came to me in every possible way I could. I have greatly modified my goals since then. I have become a great respecter of timing when it comes to change, realizing that what I might think is the proper area to change at this time is in fact not the proper sequence at all.

## Summary

For the Christian, dramatic change is a way of life. Having passed spiritually from death to life, Christians expect to see relationships altered in the lives of the believing community.

People go to counselors seeking change. But frequently they do not understand all that needs to change; they merely want relief from symptoms.

When a counselor deals in second-order change, he witnesses a reordering of a relationship with its accompanying transformation of perspective—a restructuring of the map on the right side of the brain. As we begin to talk more about how relationships are set up and function and how we change them, primarily second-order change will be considered.

## Notes

[1]Joseph Alleine: quoted in William James, *Varieties of Religious Experience* (New York: Mentor, 1958), 185.

[2]Jonathan Edwards: quoted in James, *Varieties of Religious Experience*, 185.

[3]Paul Watzlawick, John Weakland, and Richard Fisch, *Change* (New York: Norton, 1974), 10ff.

[4]Bradford Keeney, *The Aesthetics of Change* (New York: Guilford, 1983), 7.

[5]Watzlawick et al., *Change*, 23.

[6]Richard Fisch, John Weakland, and Lynn Segal, *The Tactics of Change* (San Francisco: Jossey-Bass, 1982), 127ff.

# 5
# Pacing

People who seek counseling usually feel very negative. They have little hope, having unsuccessfully tried to solve their problems. They are anxious about the counseling: "I will be blamed for all that is wrong." The counselor's first task is to make these people feel comfortable and create an atmosphere of trust and hope.

A counselor must use his observations and professional skills to make contact with each person who comes to him so that he might gain rapport—a process called "pacing." It is assumed that the Christian counselor operates from a position of unconditional love, realizing that although all are fallen, all people are God's creation. *Agape* love springs from the heart of the lover in gratitude for the love received. It is not set in motion by the object loved merely because that object is so lovable.

Just as Jesus was able to move smoothly and quickly into a personal dialogue with the woman at the well, a counselor needs the skills to be able to gain this type of rapport quickly. He needs the ability to step into another person's world to a degree, note the person's perspective, and use elements of the perspective to help the person know he is understood. The perspective, or worldview, is the map that person has. The map has some elements that can be considered cultural and some that can be considered emotional. We will look at how to pace these two elements.

Let's consider first the cultural element of the map. The

apostle Paul is apparently discussing the necessity to step into another person's world in regard to evangelism when he says:

> Though I am free and belong to no man, I make myself a slave to everyone, to win as many as possible. To the Jew I became like a Jew, to win the Jews. To those under the law I became like one under the law (though I myself am not under law), so as to win those under the law. To those not having the law I became like one not having the law (though I am not free from God's law but am under Christ's law), so as to win those not having the law. To the weak I became weak, to win the weak. I have become all things to all men so that by all possible means I might save some (1 Cor. 9:19–22).

Paul is not talking about a compromise in his basic doctrinal stance or his ethics. He is talking about accommodating to people in their unique cultural settings—which can be seen as segments of the individual's map that are shared by the wider population—motivated by love, so that he might better lead them to the gospel.

When people talk to a counselor, they articulate their problems by using their maps. We said in the chapter on communication how difficult it is to ascertain meaning from another person as they represent their experiences in words. We all think we know what the other person is saying, but we attach meaning to the words from our own maps and tend to get confused as to what is actually happening. But we are getting ahead of ourselves and must wait to discuss this in more detail later.

Pacing means stepping into another person's world for a moment, meeting the person there to let him know that we are truly "with him," and then leading him in the direction of change. A person will not follow a counselor or a confidant in the direction of change—especially second-order change, which is difficult to bring about anyway—unless he is certain that the counselor or confidant is really understanding him and is "for" him.

Consider what we said in the chapter on observing. People who agree get into "sync" with each other by mirroring each other's posture, rate of delivery, tone, and so on. This is what pacing entails, for in pacing we match the verbal and nonverbal behaviors of the other person so that the person senses (right side) that we are in "sync" with him and have entered their world and truly understand.

The second element we find as we get into a person's world is the emotional component of the map. We see this expressed in Romans 12:15: "Rejoice with those who rejoice; mourn with those who mourn." As we encounter the myriad experiences of life, certain emotional responses emerge. If we go to a person who is mourning and our attitude is one of rejoicing, that other person will want to get away from us as quickly as possible, for he will know we really don't understand what he is enduring. A strong bond is formed, however, when we are able to match up with a person, for he will know that we are sharing his experience. Being with a person emotionally is called "empathy."

Whether we are counselors or people seeking to improve a relationship, we need to be congruent—our words must match our nonverbal communication. Lacking this quality, we will have a difficult time gaining rapport with a person. If we say that we love unconditionally, that we accept a person for who he is as God's creation, then we had better communicate this on all levels. Pacing will not be effective if it is not done congruently. In fact, there is the danger that our pacing will become a manipulative trick if it does not spring from a heart of genuine concern.

There are two types of pacing: verbal and nonverbal. Both can be used powerfully to gain rapport with people as a prelude to helping them change.

## Verbal Pacing

In verbal pacing, statements are made that match the person's inner experience (their map) and to which the person will readily agree. Consider several examples.

### Example 1

You go to the home of a woman whose husband has just died. She is in tears and is greatly distressed. You sit down with her and make several pacing statements:

"It hurts terribly inside right now, doesn't it?"

"I'll bet you feel as if the hurt will never go away."

"Added to the hurt is that awful sense of loss."

These are all common feelings of a person who has lost someone close. In hearing these things said, he feels understood. In regard to death and bereavement, many of us feel upset, somewhat threatened (even in Christian contexts), and uncomfortable while trying to talk with those who mourn. Consequently, we may make ill-timed or erroneous statements:

"We can rejoice knowing your husband is much better off in heaven."

"You shouldn't feel so bad. Jane is no longer feeling all that pain."

Death in a Christian context involves two separate messages that should always be kept in mind. For the Christian, death is a door. When entered, the door leads into the presence of God; therefore there is rejoicing. This is one part of the message. But death is also the enemy (1 Cor. 15:26). When our loved one walks through that door, he is separated from us, causing our sadness and sense of loss. Yet Paul says that we don't grieve like those who have no hope (1 Thess. 4:13). Death involves grief for the Christian, for there is separation and loss. But the grief is filled with hope.

*Example 2*

Hospital situations are notorious for the absence of pacing. A nurse comes in with a two-foot-long needle to give you a shot and says, "Relax, this won't hurt a bit." So when that needle hits your skin, that nurse has lost all credibility. This exposes an interesting point: we pace to gain credibility. When we are able to articulate what matches the other person's experience, we build our believability. That person then will be much more willing to hear what else we have to say.

A good pace for that nurse would be something like this: "You must be nervous, anticipating how much this will hurt. It will hurt, but my experience has been that it usually doesn't hurt as much as people fear."

*Example 3*

Parents have difficulty pacing also. When their children are hurt, they tend to dismiss the pain: "Oh, it doesn't hurt that badly." Then, when the child protests that it does hurt that badly, the parent dismisses this also. By contrast, one perceptive father saw his six-year-old son fall down and cut his leg. When the father reached him, he saw that the leg was bleeding badly. He said to his son, "That hurts terribly, doesn't it? And it will probably go right on hurting for a little while." Then the father directed the boy's attention to how red the blood was, that it was good, rich, red blood. By then the child knew that his father understood the situation and his inner experience thoroughly, and he was able to do as his father instructed.

If we make a statement about what we think another person's experience is and they reject our statement, we should not attempt to force it, because that does not work. We should attempt to make another statement that the person is able to endorse readily. Pacing is matching what is already there in the other person, not trying to force our interpretation of what is there. If we try to force it, the other person will merely assume we don't understand and will move away from us as quickly as possible.

Another part of verbal pacing has to do with matching the verbal metaphors presented. This is precisely what Jesus did in his powerful interaction with the Samaritan woman. He used the metaphor of water to convey his spiritual truth. This metaphor was easily picked up by the woman, who was involved with water right at that moment. She did have some trouble realizing that it was a metaphor (right side) and not literal water (left side). But the image was highly appropriate for her. She could quickly and easily make the identification and feel rapport with Jesus.

Perhaps some more examples will clarify how critical verbal pacing can be in many situations.

*Example 4*

A man bursts into a minister's office on Monday morning and declares, "Your sermon yesterday was terrible! It was not well prepared and was theologically inaccurate. When are you going to clean up your act?"

When anger is direct, a proper response is difficult. It is hard to stay calm and not counterattack or defend yourself. Obvious examples of nonpacing here would be:

"You think you can do any better?" (Counterattack)

"I'm so sorry. God knows I try." (Defensiveness)

Not surprisingly, sometimes one congruent, pacing sentence can disarm an attack. In this example the man has some obvious concerns. Very likely, the sermon is merely the vehicle for conveying a lot of feelings he has about a number of issues, many of which may not involve the minister at all (he doesn't like the way the board runs the church, his wife bullied him that day, he's nervous about losing his job). Verbal pacing from the minister would let the man know he is understood. Once this is accomplished, the man will know that the minister is in his world, where the two of them can commune instead of fight.

Here are some verbal pacing statements the minister might use, but he must say them congruently, not patronizingly:

"You're really fed up, aren't you?" (Notice he acknowledges the anger, but not the object at which it is directed.)

"Sometimes things just don't go right, do they?" (Again, though this is ambiguous about what hasn't gone right, it acknowledges that something has gone wrong or this man would not be in his office screaming.)

One counselor said that over the years he has attempted to get a repertoire of "pacing statements" he can use when attacked so that he won't say the wrong thing. These are critical moments when much can be won or lost by the statements exchanged. Because these situations are so emotionally charged, the likelihood someone will mishandle them increases; therefore the need to have a sense of how to pace at these critical times is very important.

We should try to keep in mind that when a vehement attack comes our way that seems unwarranted for the degree of the offense, our attacker is undoubtedly responding to needs and feelings that go far beyond the issue at hand (process over content). We want to get to the real issues, but we can't if we "nail" him when he attacks us.

*Example 5*

A woman is very upset when she comes to a counselor. She cannot sit in her chair as she explains her situation. She gets up, paces the floor, and wrings her hands as she continues to repeat, "I just don't know what I'm going to do! Twenty years of marriage, and he leaves me for another woman. Just walks out on me and the kids."

Many counselors would try to calm down this woman, using a tranquil voice and soothing words:

> "It'll be all right. You still have Jesus with you."

> "Please try to settle down. Here, sit here and tell me about it."

When the counselor says such things, the woman knows that he obviously doesn't understand her pain and hurt. If he did, how could he say it will be all right? Asking an agitated person to sit down when he or she is very anxious and upset is usually ill-advised. In a situation like this the counselor should act a bit anxious himself as he talks with the woman. He probably should stand up, too, as he speaks to her and maybe even walk the floor with her while saying something like, "Can you believe this has happened? Twenty years down the drain! It's incomprehensible that he would want to throw away everything for someone else. No wonder you're so upset!"

Of course, the counselor would not want to spend an entire session walking the floor. But he must get into her world first, and at this moment her world involves walking back and forth. To reiterate, the object is to meet her at this point and then, when she is with him and knows he is with her, to direct her out of the dilemma.

## Example 6

A teenager goes for counseling along with his parents. Mother and Father chatter for fifteen minutes about how bad and rebellious their son has been. His head falls lower and lower on his chest. The counselor knows that this office is the last place on earth the boy wants to be now, so he needs to pace him quickly or he will lose him completely. He can make statements about the situation that the teen can readily endorse:

> "This is miserable, being dragged here by your parents and listening to all their accusations." (Notice he doesn't cast any aspersions on the parents or their authority. With them sitting there it would be a "nonpace" of them, and it would undercut their authority.)

> "This is embarrassing, I'm sorry."

With teenagers in particular, it is good to do what is called "priming the pump." This is making statements about their experience that we think the teenagers will endorse. If we are wrong, the teen merely says, "That's not it," and we move on to other statements. But when the statements are on target, the teen knows that we understand. Here are some examples of statements that prime the pump:

> "Your mom and dad have never really known how bad you feel inside, have they?"
>
> "Sometimes it's hard to know if you fit in at all."

A final comment on verbal pacing: When a counselor is working with more than one person in the office, such as a couple or a family, he must be sure to pace everyone present. Rapport needs to be built *and* maintained with all participants. If this is not done, the unpaced person may sabotage the counseling.

## Nonverbal Pacing

The second type of pacing is nonverbal. Here various aspects of a person's body language are noted and mirrored, including breathing, voice tone and rate, body posture, and movements. When a counselor is pacing nonverbally, only one or two of these behaviors need to be copied. In fact, one effective way to do it is to pace one movement with another movement, only at the same rate. Let's say a person is tapping his foot. The counselor can tap his hand to the same beat. In example 5 for verbal pacing, the counselor paces the woman nonverbally by getting up and walking around as she is doing.

This nonverbal pacing happens naturally when two people agree. When a counselor does it, the client feels much more warmth from him. Not surprisingly, good counselors who exhibit a lot of warmth to their clients tend to do this automatically.

An important point is that this type of pacing is only effective if it is done unconsciously. If a person becomes aware that a counselor is mirroring some aspect of his behavior, he will attend to it consciously and the rapport will be lost.

The best place to learn nonverbal pacing is in social situations or at home with the family. We have already stated that good counselors need to be good observers. Now those observations can be employed in bringing about rapport with people. Many people who are chronically isolated and alone in our society are people who have never really learned how to pace. They are chronically out of sync with the rest of the world. Because of this they are ignored by society and experience the world as a hostile place in which to live.

## Example 7

A family with a three-year-old go to a counselor. Blocks and toys are put on the floor for the toddler. After talking with other family members about the problems, the counselor drops to his knees and begins to play blocks with the three-year-old. The counselor has assumed the eye level, posture, and activity of the child. Now that he is "in the child's world" for a moment, he may want to ask the child a question to make contact:

"Is your family a fun place to be?"

## Example 8

A woman phones a counselor to ask for marriage counseling. She complains at length about her husband and then says he is reluctant to accompany her to counseling because of a bad experience in marital counseling.

When the couple finally show up for their appointment, the counselor learns that the husband was accused by both the wife and the former counselor as being an unscriptural spouse. Obviously, the new counselor needs to win the husband's rapport. But the wife comes across as a know-it-all, and the danger is that the counselor will take the husband's side against the wife and fail to pace her. Both spouses will need the counselor's support and must sense that he has heard and understood their positions.

Consequently the counselor might turn to the husband and say, "Your wife may fail to realize how hard you've tried all these years to be a good and loving husband to her." Then he would turn to the wife and say, "But you've missed the security of knowing that he will be there for you and be strong when you need him."

It is appropriate at this point to practice some of the things we have discussed.

*Exercise 1*

Find someone who would be willing to work with you for a half-hour in an observational exercise. This person should sit near you where you can observe his face clearly.

Ask him to think of someone he likes. As he thinks, watch for small changes in his breathing, posture, muscle tone, and skin color. Next, ask him to think of someone he does not like. Again observe the various changes that are evoked. Have your partner switch back and forth between the two people in his mind until you are confident you can see the physical differences in your partner as he thinks about the two. Now ask these questions:

Who is taller?
Whom have you seen most recently?
Which one has darker hair?
Which one is heavier?
Which one lives nearer to you?

After each question, tell your partner which person you think it is. Also note that you may see some contrasting responses as the person considers the two. The answer should be the one he settles on just before he stops thinking about it.

*Exercise 2*

Ask your partner to relate to you a significant experience such as getting married or having a baby. As he or she tells this to you, pace a nonverbal behavior. After you have paced for a while, shift your position in that behavior and see if your partner will follow. As an example, match your partner's toe tapping, then try to vary the tempo and see if he or she will follow.

## Representational Systems

We live in a world dominated by words. We therefore tend to believe that our thinking is mainly accomplished in words. But thinking is basically the manipulation of memory images.[1] The greatest source of these is our senses; we literally think in sensory images. We can make mental images of tastes, sights, sounds, and feelings. This sensory thinking is a product of the right side.

One group of people interested in human behavior has taken

this idea and has considered how this sensory thinking can be used. We will only touch on the findings of these neurolinguistic programmers.[2]

These researchers have stated that when we experience data consciously we choose one sensory mode to gather the information, organize it, and express it. The sensory modes we use are the visual (seeing), the auditory (hearing), and the kinesthetic (touching). Of course, people use all three modes, but a person tends to have one in which he is more sensitive and which he will use to make the finest distinctions.

As an example, if someone asked you to remember the last concert you attended, you would go back into your memory and bring up that fact to consider. If you tend toward being a visual person, you would primarily (not totally) remember how the orchestra looked and how the hall was arranged. If you tend toward the auditory, you would remember the music played and how it sounded. If you tend toward the kinesthetic, feelings received from the experience would be foremost in your memory.

The highly visual person would translate information into a visual image to represent its meaning. This person then will rely on visual images at the expense of hearing and feeling. The hearing-sensitive person obviously would emphasize this mode, and the kinesthetic sensitive person would use the feeling mode.

It would be ideal for a person to be able to use all three modes as appropriate to various contexts. A symphony is best enjoyed if the auditory channel is primary. Driving a car requires the visual mode to take charge. Appreciating a back rub needs kinesthetic awareness. We tend to limit our experiences, however, when we force all experiences through one primary mode. It is beneficial to know a person's favored representation mode so that as we speak with him we can use the same mode, thus gaining rapport by nonverbal pacing.

There are two ways to know a person's representational system. The first is by listening to the predicates in the person's speech. The auditory person uses predicates such as *hear, sounds, told, listen, tell myself,* and *sounds like.* He will say things such as "I hear you saying that you like me." These people like to "talk over" ideas in their head as they reach decisions. As we listen to them, they will use these "hear" words, and we can use them back: "I hear what you're saying."

The visual person sees pictures in his head. When he talks, he uses words such as *see, picture, vision, seek, insight, focus, clear,* and *went blank.* He will use phrases like "I see what you are saying."

The kinesthetic person, by contrast, wants to get a feeling for information. Pictures and sounds are less valuable. As he talks, he will use words such as *feel, grasp, handle, in touch with, firm, sensitive,* and *contact.*

The other way that we can ascertain a representational mode is by watching a person's eyes. Neurolinguistic programmers say that when people are using a particular mode in their heads, their eyes will go in a certain direction. When they are looking at pictures in their heads (visual), eyes go up. In the auditory mode, eyes go back and forth. When eyes go down and to the right, the person is sensing how the body feels. Obviously it would take some practice to notice and use this information.

*Exercises*

Here are some exercises to demonstrate how the representational modes work. First, get a partner and again ask him to relate a significant experience to you such as when he became engaged or when he got married. As he relates the experience, listen for the predicates to discern what his representational mode is. When you discover it, start using it with the person as you comment on what he is saying: "I see what you mean." After you have done this for several minutes, change your predicates with your partner unexpectedly; for example, go from visual to auditory—"I hear what you are saying"—and try to observe if this has an effect on him.

Next, ask your partner several questions like those that follow. As you do, notice what he does with his eyes. After each question you can ask him how he acquired his information.

> What color is the carpet in your car?
> What color are your mother's eyes?
> On a stoplight, what color is on top?
> How would you look with purple hair?
> What would a giraffe with an elephant's head look like?

Which door in your house sounds the loudest when it is
   slammed?
What is your favorite song?
What does cat fur feel like?
What does jumping in a cold ocean feel like?
How did you feel this morning?

## Summary

Before we can lead a person into change, we must be able to
establish a relationship with him in which he can trust us and feel
understood. To do this we must be able to step into his world for a
time and give him the experience of knowing we are with him.
This type of rapport is something we all sense (right side). It is not
something that can be explained logically.

Rapport is gained as the sensitive counselor matches his verbal
and nonverbal behavior with the person to whom he speaks. As
this is accomplished, the person senses intuitively that the
counselor understands his position (even if the counselor does not
agree with it). The basic sense of understanding is essential before
the counselor can lead the person out of his difficulties.

Rapport can be gained quickly in two ways. The counselor
can "talk the person's language," making statements that match
the person's inner experience or are metaphorically connected to
his existence. Or the counselor can match behaviors so that
physically he is in sync with the other person.

## Notes

[1] Thomas R. Blakeslee, *The Right Brain* (New York: Playboy Books,
1980), 52.

[2] Neurolinguistic programming is the label given by these researchers
as they have attempted to understand and use mental processes. See
Richard Bandler and John Grinder, *The Structure of Magic*, vols. *1 and 2*
*(Palo Alto, Calif.: Science and Behavior, 1975–76).*

# Part 2
# APPLICATIONS

# 6

# Progressing

She was nicely dressed, petite, and well spoken, but it was also obvious that she was troubled. She sat in my office, eyes cast downward, and stated that her husband had just told her he wanted to leave her to date other women. This had come as a complete surprise to her. She said, "I've met his needs quite adequately over our ten years of marriage, and he's been there for me. I just don't understand."

Actually the husband had become increasingly aloof in the last year. He had also told her at one point not long ago that he wondered why she hadn't left him. This gave me an idea.

I told her to have her husband come with her the next time. He did. He told me that he had lost his sense of "specialness" to his wife when his son had been born eight years ago. At that point he felt all her attention go in that direction. In addition, he sketched a picture of a man who felt that he had never been able to meet his wife's needs adequately. I suggested, "You have never felt as if you were enough for your wife." He readily agreed.

Gradually I realized that they had never made the transition from being husband and wife to being mother and father. As she assumed the mother role with her newborn, he felt left out.

Life is filled with transitions like that one. In this chapter we will look at transitions that couples and families must negotiate, realizing that if for some reason the transition cannot be made, problems will develop.

Having learned to observe for profitable information, to listen to all channels of communication, and to gain rapport, we must now consider the particular ways in which relationships are structured and developed over time.

Through the centuries, and especially recently, researchers have studied the family to determine how it functions, what makes a normal family normal, and what actually occurs when things go wrong and symptoms develop. Most researchers agree that the family operates like all other relational systems. The basic characteristics of a family system are these:

1. The family as a whole is greater than the sum of the parts. The family as a relating unit cannot be explained and understood simply by looking at all the members of the family individually and adding up their individual characteristics.

2. A change in one family member affects changes in the other members and the family as a whole. The behavior of the members of the family is interlocked, thus blurring the distinctions we are used to when we try to say, "This caused that."

3. All behavior in a family has value as communication or has the quality of being a message.

4. Unspoken, unwritten rules guide family behavior (the family map).

5. Families struggle to stay stable while simultaneously managing great changes that confront them.

Taking the family as a whole, we will look at two important dimensions: time (process) and space (structure). These two dimensions coexist, yet it is very difficult to deal with them together. Unfortunately, we give up important data when one dimension is emphasized over the other.

The whole thrust of the Bible is that man is inherently relational. In formulating theology and psychology, we must find words that display man in relationship, the fact that he exists simultaneously as a whole entity unto himself while at the same time as a part of a larger whole. We must also be able to see how relationships develop over time, the changes that occur, and the problems that develop.

Erik Erikson wisely pointed out the cycles that individuals pass through from birth to death, cycles that are regulated by society. He said that as the individual passes through a stage, there is a critical issue that must be successfully negotiated so that he can continue his development—e.g., the infant must learn to trust.

As people began to look at families as whole entities, it became apparent that families also pass through time and in the process encounter various developmental tasks that must be met and handled. If these tasks are not dealt with, symptoms develop at key milestones in a family's development. In other words, if a family comes to a stage of life where something is supposed to happen and doesn't (e.g., a child reaches adulthood and is supposed to leave home, but stays until well into middle age), or something that isn't supposed to happen does (e.g., a fourteen-year-old runs away from home), trouble ensues. Family developmental stages usually involve someone's entering the family (marriage, birth) or someone's leaving the family (death, children growing up and going on their own).

A number of different lists of stages exist, but the one developed by Jay Haley is particularly noteworthy.[1] His system includes six stages, as follows.

## Courtship

Courtship is the time of life when the child shifts from being a juvenile to being an adult. At this time the child must establish a separate identity. It is hoped that he is determining his particular gifts, abilities, and strengths. Also, it is appropriate that a sense of vocation take root at this time.

Throughout the child's life the parents have been turning more and more responsibility over to him—letting him go for walks on his own, feeding himself, developing bathroom and grooming rituals. Then it comes time for the parents to let the child go, handing over the reins to him. But this turning over of responsibility involves more than just physical needs.

Separation from the family involves an emotional detachment that is absolutely critical to mature development. The bonds that have kept the family together must now be loosened enough to permit the grown child to leave the family and establish himself in the community. Once into the community, the young adult must be able to launch a career and establish a social standing. He must also be able to relate in intimate ways with nonfamily people.

Success at this stage is achieved as the person is able to overcome personal inadequacies, associate appropriately with people his own age, achieve adequate status in his segment of society, and above all, disengage from his family of origin. Once these have been accomplished, the person is ready to move on to the next developmental stage.

Probably the most telling examples of young people having trouble negotiating this stage are those who are unable to find mates (not those who actively seek singleness) because of certain inadequacies. A counselor recalls working with a young woman in her mid-twenties who was attractive and well-employed. She could have had almost any man she wanted. But whenever an eligible, interested man turned up, she ignored him. She had attached herself to several married men in destructive, long-term liaisons that kept her from finding a suitable young man. It seemed that part of her was frightened of intimacy and long-term commitment, so the only choice was to attach herself to ineligible—and thus less threatening—men.

Many young people emerge from the tumult of adolescence with poor physical self-images, some to the point where they fear no one would ever accept them. Some have difficulty with weight control and proper grooming; others have attractive bodies but internal maps that say they are in fact ugly. Sometimes the difficulties are so severe that the person will not seek a dating relationship until something drastic is done.

Others are concerned about sexual orientation. Many young people of either sex wonder if they are homosexual. Some say they have been haunted by thoughts and feelings about persons of their own sex. For many this proves to be a normal developmental stage through which they pass. For others the concerns are real.

Still others have less profound concerns, though they are no less painful. A college senior was petrified when it came to talking with females. Even though he functioned well at school, he had become extremely anxious that he was not able to deal appropriately with the opposite sex, especially since many of his friends were considering marriage.

Another example of the young person who cannot get

through this period and move on with his life is one who remains at home, is dependent on parents, and is either unemployed or underemployed. Jay Haley has postulated that these young people serve to stabilize an unstable family situation, diverting attention from the real areas of conflict.[2] Usually families take such young people into counseling when there is concern that they are not keeping up with their peers. Either they have dropped out of college, or they have moved around from job to job. In any case, they are not doing what they should. Usually one parent is more detached and also insistent that the person hurry and get on with his life.

Some people are able to find potential mates, but then they have courtships that go on interminably. A counselor worked with a couple who had dated for ten years; they were then in their mid-thirties. Both were well-established in careers, but whenever the subject of marriage arose, the man froze. There was something about his fiancée and the thought of committing to her that positively frightened him, even though he was unaware of what it was.

When a young person is able to complete this developmental stage, he is ready for the next stage—marriage.

## Marriage

The Bible has much to say about the marital stage of development in the family. There is no society on earth that does not recognize a marriage ceremony of some sort. The Bible begins immediately with marriage, establishing it as the basic social institution. In Genesis 2:24 we see the basic ingredients of marriage: the male person leaves his family, he cleaves to his spouse, and then the two become one flesh.

This simple formula is really quite profound, for if any of these elements is excluded, the marriage will struggle for survival. The first element is leaving the parents. Fortunately, all cultures have a ceremony to mark the occasion of marriage so that the individuals who are the prospective couple can cross over a clear line of demarcation. This helps everyone—the couple, their families of origin, and the society—make the shift to new ways of relating to the newly formed unit.

Marriage, it must be remembered, is the joining of two

persons *and* the joining of two families. There is a tremendous
loyalty shift for the couple away from their original families and
toward each other. Humans are the only creatures who have in-
laws, and the confusing interplay within kinship networks can be
very baffling for all concerned. As marriage looms, it is to be hoped
that there has been a substantial leaving of the original families to
permit the couple to work out the second element.

It is probably unrealistic to think that anyone has become
completely emotionally independent from his family of origin.
However, many young married couples have particular difficulty.
Some couples are forced to depend on in-laws for financial support
or housing. Many times these needs are fulfilled with strings
attached. But there are also situations in which couples cannot
move off in any direction until in-laws are consulted. Battle lines
can easily be drawn as old alliances are maintained.

A young woman had been married several times. In each case
her close relationship with her father had been an insurmountable
problem to the couple. The father was always ready to be her
advocate when the conflicts erupted in the marriage. The husbands
found themselves on the periphery, competing for the wife's loyalty
and attention.

Marriage is not only leaving, but also cleaving. Remember
what we said about the map of reality that each of us carries in the
right side of the brain. This map has been developed during all our
years growing up. It contains our unique perspectives on experience—how we should act, what roles we should play, our attitudes
and values at the deepest levels of our existence. As a couple come
together in marriage, two maps are unconsciously spread out on the
table and the negotiations begin.

Unfortunately, few couples realize that they are engaged in a
discussion regarding their internal maps. They are unaware of
many of the most important sections of these. Regardless, the
discussions and struggles begin in earnest.

Clifford Sager likes the metaphor of contracts.[3] It is as if the
couple take their maps unconsciously and from them forge a
marriage contract that contains all the expectations they have for
each other. Some of the clauses in the contract are conscious and
spoken to the partner: "I want you to be totally faithful to me."
Some are conscious but not discussed: "It really scares me when

you spend so much time away with your friends; I feel unimportant." But the truly powerful clauses remain unconscious; therefore they are never really analyzed and discussed.

Sager delineates some of these major issues that can haunt a couple for a lifetime, as follows:

1. How independent or dependent should we expect each other to be? Do I want my spouse to be totally dependent on me for every need? Do I want to lean on my spouse for everything? Or do we forge relatively independent lives?

2. How close should we get? Can I really "open up" and be vulnerable with my mate? (Monica McGoldrick says that many couples confuse closeness with fusion. The person who seeks fusion is the person who wants to complete himself in another person, in effect, to fill in the missing pieces of his own sense of self and esteem.[4] This is vastly different from the person who has reasonable security within his own identity while seeking to be close with another and sharing life together with that other person.)

3. How active or passive will I be in this relationship? Will I initiate most of the action, or let my mate take the lead most of the time?

4. Who will submit (be "one-down") and who will dominate (be "one-up")? Will this vary between us at certain times and in certain tasks? Or will one be primarily one-up and the other one-down all the time?

5. How severe are my fears that I will be abandoned by the other and have to be alone? How do I handle these fears?

6. How do I feel about myself as a man or a woman? What are my expectations as to how my spouse should act as a person of the opposite sex?

After the couple leave and cleave, they are to become one flesh. This of course involves a sexual bonding. But there is also a "one-fleshness" that is a much deeper bonding, and it comes as a result of the two partners' beginning to forge a common map of reality. This map develops from the two separate maps each person brings to the marriage, containing their individual perspectives on life, love, intimacy, sex roles, and so on. The individual will experience more intensity in some areas than in others because of basic issues that have been left unresolved.

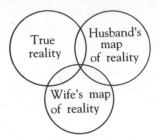

Figure 6.1: **Interaction of Spouses' Maps of Reality**

As we can see in figure 6.1, parts of the maps of the couple overlap with reality. In some places the maps overlap each other but not with true reality, and these areas are problematic and intense because both partners' perceptions of them are distorted.

Some theorists suggest that the residue of past unsatisfactory relationships—especially with parents—lies within the folds of the map, waiting to resurface in the person of the spouse so that old, festering issues can be reworked. Each partner then sets up the other partner to act like this someone with whom they are familiar and with whom there is still unresolved internal conflict or intensity.

At any rate, certain issues begin to emerge for the couple in matters where both partners experience intensity. Let's say that John and Sue marry. Both have buried in their maps the thought that control of the relationship is a problem area. As she was growing up, Sue saw her father drink and act very irresponsible, squandering the family's money. "I'll never let this happen in my family," she said to herself.

John, however, had a mother who was forceful and overbearing. She constantly wanted to know everything he did, monitoring his phone calls and opening and reading his mail. When John decided to start his own business, Sue became anxious about the family finances and began to badger John and to monitor all his business dealings. John responded by withdrawing, remembering the pain of an overbearing woman in his life. This made Sue even more anxious as she remembered her father's withdrawing into alcohol in his attempts to deal with his inadequacies.

Since then, both John and Sue have accessed each other's maps in a very powerful and negative way. Sue now "sees" John as the irresponsible man withdrawing from his problems; John "sees" Sue as the overbearing woman trying to run his life.

Virtually all couples face numerous areas in their maps that are more or less mutually problematic. Yet some couples are able to deal with these issues much more quickly and skillfully than others. The difference appears to be the particular personal strength (or lack thereof) that each member brings to the marriage.

Virginia Satir likes to pose this individual strength as a person's self-esteem. When a person has low self-esteem, he bases his evaluations to an extreme extent on what others think. His dependence cripples his ability to function independently and effectively, but instead of seeking help he masks his difficulties.[5]

Of course, esteem is not an individual matter; it is always chiseled out in relationship. The person of low self-esteem, Murray Bowen points out, is a person still bound in negative ways to his own family.[6] Unfortunately, people tend to choose mates with similar degrees of self-esteem. The people low on the scale who marry others low on the scale hope to find in their mates the qualities they sense lacking in themselves. When they cannot find them in the other person, disappointment sets in and the couple cling more tightly to each other, hoping somehow to complete what is lacking. These couples have a great deal of difficulty overcoming intense areas in their relationship successfully, for they have little energy to give to the task. Most of their energy is used up in just hanging on to their fragile senses of themselves.

Many newlyweds feel somewhat shattered after having their first fight. They feel certain that this traumatic event means that their marriage is over. Such couples have never known what healthy disagreement is. In regard to conflict, they have only two speeds: Off and High. A counselor's job is to help them learn how to disagree effectively and come mutually to decisions that are satisfying to both.

As time goes by, the couple who are not able to deal effectively with conflicted areas of their relationship begin to slip into recurring patterns of interaction around the issue. As they go round and round, they begin to see each other as one-dimensional. Although God made humans magnificently complex, the embattled couple look at each other only in one or two negative traits that appear to be continually reconfirmed: "John is always thoughtless"; "Sue is just a shrew." Regardless of what a person does, it is used as proof that the negative trait is still present.

As this stage of development draws to a close, the couple have hammered out some type of mutual map or contract between them. Some couples divorce during the first year of marriage because they are totally unable to formulate this mutual map. But those who do assimilate their maps move on to the next stage.

### Dealing With Childbirth and the Young

When the first child comes along, a triangle is immediately created—where once there were two, now there are three. If the couple have been able to adjust to one another successfully, it increases the likelihood of a smooth transition into the triangle. One hopes that the couple have been able to negotiate a workable marital map that can adequately meet the needs of both.

The mutual map guiding the marriage has to give way to a new map when a child arrives on the scene. This family map, like its predecessors, will be used to give direction to everyone involved as to who does what, when, and how. Naturally there will always be interplay between the family maps that are negotiated and the individual maps that are still in everyone's right brain.

Like the other maps, this family map is unspoken, is largely out of awareness, and is virtually never taken out for close scrutiny unless a professional happens to come into the family. But the map is drawn from innumerable clauses:

"Girls never do those things."

"We will be quiet and never speak during meals."

"Men are basically impotent wimps in this family."

"Money buys all the important things in life."

"The only road to true fulfillment is by . . . (marrying, having a good job, earning a Ph.D., having children).

"Never let anyone think poorly of you; it reflects on your parents' image."

The map gives the family the "proper" perspective on all aspects of life. It begins to develop even as the first child develops in the womb. Its various clauses will be added, rearranged, and deleted as the years pass.

When the first baby arrives, many couples still face much unresolved conflict. Perhaps the husband has been very insecure and has needed a great deal of attention from his spouse. When the baby comes, the wife's attention is diverted and the husband may begin to feel abandoned. For other couples the birth of the child is a signal to in-laws to come rushing in from "stage left" and begin giving dicta to the new parents. Wives who have been strong through the early years of marriage may now want to be needy and lean on their husbands. If the husbands are not up to the task, serious problems develop.

One family theorist has discussed how unstable a relationship between two people can be, especially when there is conflict.[7] As the intensity rises, the tendency is to bring in another person so that the stress is less intense on the warring factions. A new child on the scene in the midst of a marriage in conflict provides just the right ingredient for this.

Some people marry when the woman is already pregnant. Others enter already existing families as stepparents. In each case, the couple is in a "triangled" situation from the start. This does not necessarily spell doom to the couple trying to work out differences, but it adds an extra responsibility that must be successfully met.

At any rate, a whole group of new roles must be learned. First, there are the new parents who are no longer just husband and wife. Now they must adjust to being father and mother. New mothers may have always looked forward to the rewards of parenting, but may now find the realities of daily struggles with little children more a burden than a delight. New fathers may not have a clue as to how to interact successfully at different developmental stages with their children.

Assuming parenting roles needs to progress adequately. Mothers' roles are more obvious. Recent research, however, has uncovered the importance of the father in the life of the child. The father is the one who brings legitimacy to the child; he is also the primary one to teach initiative. His endorsement of the child's strengths and his acceptance of the child's individuality are crucial.

But many men have never known much nurturing and care-giving. When their turn comes at parenting, they feel very inadequate.

For example, some new parents frantically called a counselor late one evening. They reported that their ten-month-old child had never slept through the night and tended to stay up for hours while the exhausted, distraught parents took turns nurturing her and feeding her, hoping to get her back to sleep. The counselor suggested that the baby had never learned to go to sleep on her own. They took his advice, they left the baby for a while before attending to her, and the problem was resolved in two nights.

As children arrive, many men become more absent, spending more time at work and in other pursuits. Men don't like the feelings of inadequacy that they may experience at home in the father role. They prefer the less painful, more satisfying arenas outside the home.

Of course, one of the biggest issues to surface during this time is disagreement over child-rearing practices. One typical pattern is the mother who begins to side with the child against the overly harsh father, who then becomes more peripheral. Naturally this cycle becomes self-perpetuating: as the father gets harsher, the mother hovers over the "abused" child—each parent eliciting a negative response from the other.

Grandparents and aunts and uncles are created by the birth of a child. This presents new demands in the extended family as alliances are forged between generations, visitation is negotiated, and old memories and feelings resurface in new settings to disrupt normal functioning.

Probably the problem area that looms largest is the grandparents. It is to be hoped they can be used as consultants as the new mother and father figure out how to parent. Unfortunately, many grandparents get into the middle of the parenting fray, criticizing their children for ineffectiveness. In some cases only one of the new parents is the target. Either way, the results can be very destructive.

Grandparents can also cause quite a stir by allying themselves with a grandchild against the parents. All of us have seen instances of children acting very unruly with the tacit endorsement of a grandparent; we will discuss this further in the next chapter.

Jay Haley points out that the coming of children is a time of life during which the couple must forge new commitments. Doubts that have simmered under the surface vis-à-vis the permanence of the marriage now boil to the surface. It is common for counselors to encounter tearful new mothers who have been abandoned by husbands who simply could not adjust to the new demands placed on them.

It is hoped, however, that during this period, the couple are able to adjust to the new roles of parents while at the same time keeping themselves firmly in place as husband and wife. Some couples will find that the foundations of challenges and difficulties are laid in this stage but do not surface until the next stage.

## Middle Marriage Difficulties

Remember, the task of parents is to work themselves out of a job. For some this happens fairly smoothly. As the child grows, he spends more and more time in the presence of others outside the home. Parents sense that they have handed over their children to outsiders and as a result have given up some of their ability to protect and guide them. Children come in contact with peers, teachers, and other adults who have values that conflict with the values taught in the home.

Many families encounter problems as the children begin to relate to the outside world. The child's task is to make his way into the world and find a place in it. He will no longer be accepted merely because he is a member of the family. Now what he can achieve will determine his status.

One common problem is the child who becomes "school phobic," refusing to go to school. There are many causes for this, but sometimes a family is ambivalent about the child's going to school in the first place. Perhaps that child has been most important back home as a companion to the mother. As the child enters school, the mother feels alone and depressed. The child develops "symptoms" about going to school, and the end result is that he is allowed to stay home with mother.

Other problems can develop in the outside world. Some of these involve peer relationships. Perhaps the child cannot make friends easily or gains friends who are unacceptable to the parents. It is important that the child begin to have a sense of belonging in the larger world, feeling accepted in his society.

Another whole set of problems can develop in the classroom. Some children have difficulty behaving in this setting. Other children have a problem performing classroom tasks. Professionals are left with the task of deciding whether the child has "emotional" problems and can't handle the situation, or has "learning disabilities." Because these categories are not clear and foolproof, parents may experience years of frustration dealing with school officials and other professionals attempting to get the help their children need.

As the children move through the grade school years, a new challenge looms on the horizon. Actually several important issues begin to converge at once, causing a great deal of upset to the unsuspecting family.

The first issue is the time of life we now call "mid-life crisis." For the husband, he is either finding success at work or is beginning to realize he won't attain the goals he has sought for many years. His sense of himself and his status in the eyes of his wife can suffer greatly. Added to this is the awareness that he is no longer physically what he once was. Many men then experience a sense that this moment is the last chance to grab for those lifelong dreams. To some this involves radical occupational changes. Still other men reach for youth by abandoning families and going after younger women.

The wife also is going through changes. She must begin to contend with a body that is ceasing to function the way it once did. There is also the realization that her job as mother, which may have been central to her, is diminished and nearing termination. She questions what her new role will be. She also questions whether she is important to her family any longer.

At the same time this is going on, many parents find their own parents beginning to collapse back on them for support. Many parents are reaching the age where they need much more emotional or physical support from their children. They place demands on their children right when the children are facing their own mid-life adventures.

Completing these challenges, the children reach adolescence and in many cases annihilate the family tranquility—or what there was left of it. Interestingly, the adolescent and the mid-life adult are searching for the same thing: "identity." The child is struggling to reach adulthood with its rewards and responsibilities while attempting to figure out just who he is as a person. Parents are struggling to adjust to new demands for freedom from the child and sometimes from an all-out assault on family hierarchy. The mother finds herself in competition with a daughter blossoming into womanhood. The father may find himself caught in the middle between two warring females. Sons are reaching toward manhood, placing new demands on parents to compensate and adjust. It is hoped that the parents and children are able to shift in their dealings with each other so that the children are ready to move out of the family successfully.

Old marital patterns that have festered may now burst into the open. Many of these patterns involve rigid ways of dealing with each other that have never proved satisfactory to either mate. Many couples turn to professionals to help resolve differences, only to find the patterns so entrenched that even the professionals cannot unravel the mix-ups. Divorce has increasingly become an option for unhappy, unsatisfactory relationships.

With divorce come new family constellations—single-parent families and blended families—with unique difficulties.

### Launching the Children Into the World

Children leaving the family present problems to varying degrees. Many difficulties center on new people entering the family and other people leaving.

Our society lacks the important initiation rite that clearly delineates when a child enters adulthood. Other societies have had particular ceremonies and "rites of passage" to mark this critical transition, declaring to the entire community that where once there was a child now stands an adult.

With the demands of the technological society, childhood and its schooling drag on for years. The child may find himself well into his twenties before he is completely independent from parents (in contrast with our great-grandparents, most of whom were self-supporting and married when they completed puberty).

What develops between parents and young adults is a "never-never land" of competing needs and responsibilities. As an example, a twenty-one-year-old college graduate returns home to attend graduate school. Parents still support this adult while he is in school. When the young person moves back home, the parents are shocked to find that he has acquired several values that they find distasteful. Do the parents insist that the young adult assume their values while he is living under their roof?

Other problems develop for the young person who is supposed to leave home but doesn't, or goes off to college only to return to the family after several months. In many instances, the child has been an important bridge in dealing with conflicts between parents (the triangling idea mentioned earlier). His removal from the family may prove disastrous to the well-being of the parents, whose relationship has been tenuous for years. Many children remain home virtually forever, keeping the focus of the family firmly fixed on their problems. At times these youth develop chronic legal or psychiatric problems that involve the appropriate authorities.

If a child remains home long after his time to leave has come, disagreements inevitably erupt between parents as to how best to deal with him. A classic response is for one parent to move to protect the child as the other seeks to throw him out of the house. Sometimes the parents switch roles in this endless game. However, the results are always the same: the child stays.

Problems that reach extremes in either direction tend to indicate the same problem with a different face. Therefore, the child who leaves home angry, vowing never to contact his parents again, and the child who never leaves home are both dealing with essentially the same conflict. Both are finding it hard to cut the emotional bonds and separate from their families. (The one who never contacts his family again is, curiously, still very much bound to his family in a negative way.)

For the child who leaves home successfully, both parents and child must learn to relate to each other as peers more than anything else. Many families make this transition smoothly, as it has been occurring throughout adolescence.

Parents whose children have moved out face new challenges. They are left by themselves without children standing between. This time is often referred to as the "empty nest syndrome." And it is a time when the marital map must be changed—sometimes radically. Many couples have used their children for virtually all communication. Some women have defined themselves only in terms of motherhood. Major changes must now be worked out. For many couples there is the rude and alarming discovery that they no longer have anything in common and essentially have nothing left to say to each other. Often a divorce ensues.

Other couples are able to make the transition with less difficulty. New experiences of intimacy and sharing may be the result. Some must learn to be grandparents, and this may require striking a delicate balance of participating in their children's lives without becoming overinvolved. All too often grandparents are drawn into the families of their children in inappropriate ways with much bickering and bitterness resulting. Haley points out that each generation depends on other generations in very complex ways about which we know little.[8] Obviously there are many hidden bonds and loyalties that can greatly humble a counselor who tries to tinker with these relationships.

## Retirement and Old Age

Many things can be said about our technological age. One reality is that with the emphasis on function, things and people that can't perform well tend to be devalued and discarded. As people reach retirement age, new demands are placed on them in a society that does not value this status very highly.

For a husband there is not only the loss of his job, but also perhaps the loss of the definition of "self." In a technological society, function determines identity and worth, and when one has no function, it follows that identity and worth become marginal. The husband may find himself lapsing into depression, feeling useless and hopeless.

For the wife, who possibly has leaned on her husband for many years, finding him needy and depressed may come as a shock. Even in less severe circumstances, husbands and wives who are in each other's presence for twenty-four hours a day need to rework their relationship.

Declining health is a factor that comes to the foreground as time goes on. As the years pass, one or the other spouse must deal with the death of the partner and the accompanying grief. Some come to terms with this rather quickly, while others languish in the memories and never really recover from the loss.

The younger generations must find appropriate places for their aging parents. At this stage, many younger people are attempting to find a balance between overinvolvement and detachment in dealing with elderly parents. In the best of circumstances, the younger generation is able to use the older generation appropriately as consultants in the very difficult tasks of handling life in general and raising children in particular.

## Summary

The family, seen as a whole unit, develops over time and passes through various predictable stages. These stages tend to be marked by someone either entering the family (birth, marriage) or leaving the family (death, grown children). At each stage the family must confront and successfully negotiate certain issues. Problems develop in the family because things that are supposed to happen at a certain stage do not happen, or things that aren't supposed to happen in fact do occur.

Crises predictably develop when people enter or leave the family, for it is at these times that the demands to change and adjust are the greatest. A counselor must always keep in mind where the family is in time as he begins to explore its particular structure.

## Notes

[1] Jay Haley, *Uncommon Therapy* (New York: Norton, 1973), 41ff.

[2] Jay Haley, *Leaving Home* (New York: McGraw-Hill, 1980), 79ff.

[3] Clifford Sager, *Marriage Contracts and Couple Therapy* (New York: Brunner/Mazel, 1976), 1–3.

[4] Monica McGoldrick, *The Family Life Cycle* (New York: Gardner, 1980), 96–97.

[5] Virginia Satir, *Conjoint Family Therapy* (Palo Alto, Calif.: Science and Behavior, 1967), 8.

[6] Murray Brown, *Family Therapy in Clinical Practice* (New York: Aronson, 1978), 75.

[7] Haley, *Uncommon Therapy*, 54.

[8] Ibid., 63.

# 7

# Structuring

Isaac was old, bedridden, and blind. He knew his time on earth was short, so he called in his older son Esau and asked him to fetch some wild game, prepare it, and bring it home. At that time Isaac would extend to him his blessing.

As Isaac said these things to his son, wife Rebekah was listening at the door. She quickly ran off to her favorite son, Jacob, Esau's twin brother, and devised a way for Jacob to cheat his brother out of this blessing. Rebekah had Jacob kill two goats. She prepared from them a tasty meal and used the skins to transform Jacob into a hairy man like his brother. Jacob then went to his father and succeeded in tricking him to receive the blessing intended for Esau.

This story from Genesis 27 is a vivid illustration of a family torn apart, the basic family structure having been shattered. Family members had sided one against the other—the mother pulling a son into an alliance against her husband and the other son.

Family problems are as old as families, dating to the sibling rivalry of Cain and Abel. In the previous chapter we considered how a family develops over time and what difficulties can occur during particular stages in time (the horizontal dimension). In this chapter we will look at the types of problems that can arise in the family structure (the vertical dimension).

These two dimensions are always present, of course. Each family exhibits a particular structure at a particular time in its development. These dimensions constantly interact, making it impossible in a practical sense to speak of one without considering the other.

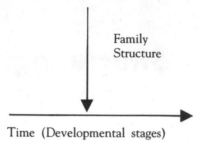

Figure 7.1: **Dimensions of Relationships**

Consider the way a family is put together. One well-known theorist has said, "A family is a system that operates through transactional patterns . . . of how, when and to whom to relate."[1] Here is a group of people related to each other who repeatedly act toward each other in the same ways. If one knows what to look for, a redundant pattern of acting will always emerge in a family. This pattern constitutes the family's structure.

In the previous chapter we mentioned the emergence of the family map as husband and wife become parents. This unconscious, unspoken map sets the rules for behavior, presupposing a certain structure or pattern of actions for each family member and for the family as a whole as it relates to itself and the world. The map sets the course for the structure, which in turn helps to remold the map over time.

The family map regulates family behavior as well as individual development. Certain aspects of the child's behavior are reinforced (shy, outspoken, aggressive, quiet, tentative). Other aspects are discouraged, thus distinguishing the individual map from the family map. The family meets with new situations and is called on to react in certain ways. The map gives perspective and direction in all these situations. (One of the hardest concepts to grasp in working with relationships is that each individual is a whole entity with his own map guiding his behavior, while simultaneously integrating his map into larger wholes, such as family, church, and community. Of course, there is always the dynamic interplay between the individual map and the corporate map, each shaping the other. This is discussed by Salvador Minuchin.)[2]

It is appropriate to take a look at the particular elements making up the family structure. We will examine subsystems, boundaries, and hierarchy within the family.

## Subsystems

The family as a whole is segmented into smaller units through which it actually carries on its business. There are three subsystems to discuss: spousal, parental, and sibling.

### The Spousal Subunit

First is the spousal subunit. We have discussed how the husband and wife come together in marriage. That union forms the basic subunit that begins the family. For obvious reasons it is a critical component in the whole structure of the family. As the husband and wife come together, there is a sense of specialness between them, a feeling that they are vitally important to each other without the intrusion of in-laws, children, friends, or outside interests.

When they have children, one of the chief tasks of the couple is to model for their offspring what an intimate relationship is all about. Intimacy involves many factors, but certainly it is the coming together of two persons in a shared relationship where there is openness and honesty as to who each is as a person. Genesis 2:25 is a powerful statement about true intimacy: "The man and his wife were both naked, and they felt no shame."

Intimacy involves vulnerability, and it is here that a couple begin to balk at the idea of openness. When a person is open and vulnerable, he is in a most defenseless and precarious position. If we reject him at that point, we are rejecting what is in a sense the "real" person. If he can keep up his defenses when we reject him, he can at least be satisfied that we have rejected only the caricature of him that he allowed us to experience.

Obviously there is never total communion between husband and wife. However, some couples are able to be much more open and intimate than others. It is to be hoped that as the years go by, the couple will vigilantly guard their relationship with one another and not let others impinge upon it, so that as the children in particular look at their parents, they will always know that before all else, their mother and father are first and foremost husband and wife.

This husband-wife relationship not only reveals intimacy to the children, but also shows them how men and women deal with each other. In the chapter on communication we said that the most powerful messages are rarely said verbally, but rather are communicated nonverbally through our whole way of behaving and acting. Many parents wonder how they can teach their children their values. The answer is simple: How can you not? Fortunately (and unfortunately), our children absorb all our values, including some that we know are undesirable. Again, our values lie in our maps, and these messages are transmitted by other than verbal channels.

When it comes to male-female relationships, children look to the spousal subunit to see how these relationships should operate. A husband and father can tell his children all day what he thinks of women and how he feels they should be treated, but in a real sense he might as well save his breath. He demonstrates his true attitude day in and day out as he interacts with his wife.

Fathers and mothers also demonstrate how stress is to be handled. When stress is applied to a person, does he become irrational and unable to cope? Are the accompanying feelings buried and denied? Are courses of action worked out by the husband and wife with each having equal input? Stress is constantly with a family to varying degrees, depending on the stage of life the family is experiencing. Families will develop particular unconscious strategies for dealing with the stress.

Parents also teach how conflict is resolved. Many people handle conflict poorly; some deny its existence. Some couples claim they have been married for twenty years with never a cross word between them. If that is true, then where has all the conflict—which surely existed—gone? Usually it lurks under the surface waiting for that "final straw," when it can come gushing out in a torrent. Other couples have a "one-speed" switch for conflict; either it's off (no conflict) or it's on "full speed." For them there is nothing in between.

For all the families described above, there is great difficulty in handling "normal" amounts of conflict, in disagreeing without being too disagreeable, or in losing control in conflict—but also in being able to repair the damage and go on from there. As children grow they need to learn how to manage conflict, how to understand its sources and courses, and how to take responsibility for its successful negotiation. In counseling situations, families often do not have a clue as to what to do with conflict. This may have a direct bearing on why a family is in counseling in the first place.

Parents serve as models for the expression of affection. How do a married couple show their love to one another? How does a father show affection to a child, especially an adolescent of the opposite sex? How does a mother display affection? Both parents demonstrate this day in and day out in thousands of small transactions with each other and with the children.

## The Parental Subunit

The second subsystem is the parental. As children come into the family, the husband and wife must shift into new roles as parents. Their primary job is to rear the children and, in so doing, to work themselves out of that job. During a child's developmental years, parents should gradually turn more and more responsibility over to him until he leaves his parents' home and establishes a home of his own.

Many things can be said about effective parenting, but there must always be a balance between nurturing, guidance, and control. Nurturing involves anything that assists in the growth process. Parents nurture in many ways, as by providing food and shelter, education, and spiritual opportunities. But parents also nurture by implanting in a growing child a sense of his uniqueness before God and of his gifts, talents, and abilities. Parents must be reasonably secure in their own sense of who they are before they can be expected to nurture effectively this sense of self in the child.

Child rearing also involves guidance, showing the way by directing or leading. Society has many pitfalls and dead ends that must be successfully maneuvered if the child is to reach maturity in one piece and in the fear of the Lord. The parental subunit is the primary guide through the labyrinth. In the technological society, many of the guidance responsibilities (education, religion, health, values clarification) have moved from the home to an institutional setting. Even Christian families more often than not see the church as the primary guide in religious instruction.

Guidance also carries with it the sense of control and restriction. Setting the limits of acceptable behavior is important as the child matures. Many parents have great difficulty arriving at age-appropriate limits. They find themselves locked in combat with each other as to what is the correct course of action. A typical scenario is a parent who perceives his partner as too strict. To compensate, he becomes too lenient, which only compels the other to become even more strict, which in turn makes him become more lenient.

As the child grows, the parents are called on to adjust their roles as guides and to reexamine their restrictions. This is especially true as the child reaches adolescence. Though it might have been true earlier, the adolescent is more than willing to question all restrictions and the fundamental role the parents play as guides. A delicate balancing act between parental authority and adolescent autonomy must now be mastered.

Of course, built into the child is the urge to explore the world and to grow as a result. However, for the child to branch out and chart new territory, there must always be the assurance that the world is a predictable place, a predictability molded and maintained initially by the parents.

A word needs to be said about authority. Authority involves the power to determine the direction of a relationship and the right to do so. As Christians we strongly believe that parents are invested with authority in their families. With this authority there is the right to command certain actions. This seems simple enough: the parents have the right to command action. However, the practical outworking of this can be far from simple.

Parents often disagree as to how authority and power should be wielded. Each parent's map may call for totally different methods in this regard—benevolent despot, autocratic ruler, and so on. Child development invariably calls for modifications in the exercise of authority. The children themselves challenge authority at various times, forcing particular responses from one parent or both.

A common problem in counseling is the difficulty of "meaning it." This is a problem whenever a child knows when one parent "means it," but does not know about the other parent. When a parent asks a child to do something, the child must know that the parent means it and is willing to back up requests with conse- quences for tasks left undone; otherwise the child will ignore the request. For one reason or another, some parents will make requests of children but never follow through appropriately when the child fails to comply.

Then there is the parent who positively "means it," who demands absolute compliance, no questions asked, throughout the child's life, including adolescence. In such a situation the child always experiences the parent as harsh and arbitrary. This type of climate readily breeds bitterness, resentment, and rebellion. A child in this situation can also be hampered in another way. If complete obedience is demanded, a child does not get a chance to make his own evaluations of his life and act on them, for good or ill. He then becomes an adult who can work well only in a highly structured situation, and this is a demoralizing handicap.

Also, parents teach a child how to relate in situations where there is unequal power. This involves accepting authority, taking and carrying through orders, and communicating his needs with those who have more control.[3] We have all experienced children who have reached adulthood never really having learned the lessons of submission and service.

## The Sibling Subunit

Last, there is the sibling subunit, or the children themselves. In this subunit, children learn how to compete, cooperate, and negotiate as they grow. It is here that children learn how allies are obtained and maintained. They also learn the whole concept of friendship.

With the development of friendships there is the sense of belonging to a group, and the rights and responsibilities of membership are gradually attained. Each child is developing a map on the right side of his brain that will guide his behavior. As he experiments with peer relationships, vital aspects of the map are confirmed. Roles and traits for the child also are solidified: "He's so shy" or "She's a real leader."

## Boundaries

The discussion of subsystems needs to go hand-in-hand with that of boundaries, for the concept of boundaries is a vital aspect of individuals, families, and family subsystems. In an individual, a boundary determines what *is you* from what *is not you*—a simple-sounding concept that can be very difficult to carry out in practice.

One way to see an aspect of this boundary is to have two persons stand facing each other six feet apart. Then have them walk toward one another and stop when they begin to feel uncomfortable. In such an event, each person will have a different stopping point. This point is like an invisible shield that tells us how close to another person we can tolerate being, and where we begin to feel our "space" is being violated.

In family contexts, boundaries are usually unspoken rules that define who participates with whom, when, and how.[4] In any case, boundaries must be clearly defined for families and individuals to function properly. We will consider boundaries in three spheres: individual, subsystem, and family.

Consider individual boundaries. When a child is born, there is a period of time when he must see others as an extension of himself. As he develops, the child begins to see that the people around him are not him and that there are boundaries around himself and them. Perhaps he senses something like, "There are parts that are me; there are parts that are not." In a good situation, parents assist the child in establishing the boundaries himself— determining what are his good and bad aspects, what are his mind, his feelings, his own gifts and abilities, and who he is as a sexual being. As the child reaches adolescence, these issues are tied together into his sense of identity: who he is and who he thinks other people think he is.

But many children have parents who themselves never had adequate help negotiating this stage of life. One vital characteristic of such children (and parents) is to take bad aspects of themselves (in their internal maps) and pin them on other people, blaming anyone and everyone for their own frustrations and inadequacies. In so doing, boundaries around each person are blurred, for if I take aspects of me and say they belong to you, confusion is created as to what is really you and what is really me. This becomes particularly marked in marriage, where each partner brings intense issues from his or her own map and imputes them to the other person.

People who have the poorest boundaries around themselves as individuals live in a world of unreality where they have great difficulty nailing down their own existence. They question their thoughts, feelings, and actions and may in fact slip into the terrible world of craziness, totally out of step with society and perhaps destined only for an institution.

This moves us into a discussion of family subsystem boundaries. In families where boundaries are weak between and within individuals, there is a "flowing together" of the members, forming one huge, undifferentiated "blob." Ideally there are firm boundaries around individual members and around the various subunits in the family. But weak individual boundaries lead to weak subunit boundaries.

When this happens, it becomes extremely difficult to tell who is in charge when, obviously, the parental subunit should be. The husband and wife frequently do not act in a special, intimate way toward each other. In fact, their actions toward each other are not particularly different from their actions toward other family members. People speak for each other in these families. There is the assumption that everyone thinks alike and feels the same in all situations. The sense of what it means to be a uniquely created individual is lacking.

The third type of boundary difficulty involves the whole family unit. Here a boundary will divide the family from the surrounding world, marking it as a special entity. The boundary around the family would permit and restrict certain information from entering or leaving the family.

Often the boundary is too rigid and the family has too little contact with the outside world to grow and develop as well as it should. While the boundary around the whole family is rigid, the boundaries around individuals and subsystems within the family are diffuse. We can picture the condition as shown in figure 7.2.[5]

We call this an enmeshed family. There is a high degree of communication among family members to the point of overinvolvement, forming the undifferentiated "blob" referred to earlier. Communication with the outside world is restricted.

In enmeshed families, movement by one member away from

the family (in growth, personal identity, and even normal separation) is perceived by the other members as a threat, and they will apply subtle pressure to restore the former situation. Even in this type of family there is a fixed organizational structure, but with a limited number of engulfing roles. There is fluidity as to who takes a particular role at a particular time (e.g., most dependent member, leader, mentally ill member), so one day the father will be in charge, but the next day the six-year-old daughter may assume command.

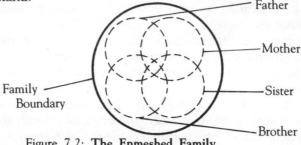

Figure 7.2: **The Enmeshed Family**

When stress hits these enmeshed families, there is a decided lack of resources available to meet the crisis. Problems can begin to develop in one or more family members. Because boundaries with the family are weak, it is difficult for anyone to take charge permanently; that role fluctuates frequently. It is also difficult to call on the outside world because the boundaries to the world are so rigid.

On the other side of the scale from the enmeshed families are the disengaged families. In these the boundary to the outside world is very loose, while boundaries between and within individuals are very rigid. These families are ruggedly individualistic to the point where only large crises can activate any support from family members. Everyone goes his own way and "does his own thing." A wide range of individual variation is tolerated and encouraged.

A disengaged family is represented in figure 7.3.

Most families fall between the extremes of the enmeshed or the disengaged. However, as a family moves toward one or the other extreme, problems usually develop in one or more family members.

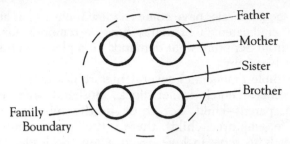

Figure 7.3: **The Disengaged Family**

Boundaries will vary in degree of rigidity in different stages of a family's development. When a mother has a newborn infant, the boundary between herself and the infant is obviously weak, and it is rigid between herself/baby and other family members. But as the child grows, the boundary that separates mother and child must grow firmer for the child to realize his individuality.

The family has the responsibility to fulfill for its members two critical needs: the need to develop a sense of personal identity ("I-ness"), and the need to relate to other human beings ("We-ness"). These two needs must always be held in balance in a family. A sense of relatedness and belonging comes as each member accommodates his assumptions and transactions to be consistent with the family. At the same time, the family must be able to accept and respect individual variations among members, seeing that each is a unique creature. The mature family teaches its members how to relate in a close, healthy way with one another while also accepting and celebrating the uniqueness and ever-increasing autonomy of each person.

## Hierarchy

As the family carries out its work, there needs to be coordination between the members to achieve what is necessary. Coordination presupposes a hierarchy, an inequality where one member or members predominate. There needs to be an "executive" or a "decider" subunit that can overrule any member and impose its will.

Probably no other concept in family sociology has been so subject to misinterpretation in both Christian and secular circles.

Many in secular circles have come to view hierarchy as an evil that must be eradicated. Christians have attempted for years to ascertain from Scripture what demands God places on his creatures regarding hierarchy.

The Bible enumerates several hierarchies that the Christian must consider: church leader—flock, husband—wife, employer—employee, parent—child. For those in the subordinate position (flock, wife, employee, child), there is the duty to stand under the leader, ready to serve in love, even when the leadership is non-Christian. For the Christian leader, there is the responsibility to act from God's point of view. Certainly the Christian leader exercises authority, but from a totally different stance than the non-Christian. Jesus discussed this point in Matthew 20:20–28. Leadership is not "lording over" people; it springs from the heart of a servant.

On this basis, hierarchy never involves a qualitative difference between the leader and the subject. Both leader and subject serve the good of the whole. Hierarchy must be maintained by *all* members of the group. If people who are higher in the hierarchy won't maintain it, then those lower down must do so.

Hierarchy is understandably a critical idea in the well-being of a family. In American society, hierarchy usually follows generational lines. Parents have the power; grandparents are at best in a peripheral role. The parents tell the children what to do, and they do it. The grandparents back up the parents and lend advice when asked for it. Regrettably, this ideal is not always achieved. Jay Haley[6] and later Cloe Madanes[7] have both stated that problems invariably arise when there is difficulty in the hierarchy. The family organization begins to unravel as hierarchical problems emerge.

Problems in the hierarchy, however, go hand-in-hand with problems in the boundaries and the subsystems. If the executive subunit (mother and father) is supposed to be running the family but isn't, that problem in hierarchy signals that the boundaries around the subunit have become shaky so that it cannot operate effectively to guide the rest of the family.

A counselor will be able to observe particular problems that involve the boundaries, subunit definition, and hierarchy of the family structure. Of course, the issues will not be discussed as boundary problems or problems with hierarchy, so the counselor has to discern these on his own. Here are some scenarios to sharpen this discernment.

*Example 1*

A mother and father take their nineteen-year-old daughter to a counselor because she has dropped out of school and is staying home doing nothing. They say her behavior is beginning to take on a "weird" quality. The family includes a ten-year-old daughter, who attends the counseling sessions. The younger girl constantly interrupts the counselor by answering all questions directed to other family members. The mother identifies strongly with the older daughter, saying she sees many of her own traits in the girl. The counselor moves to let everyone in the family answer his or her own questions and think his or her own thoughts (to set boundaries around the individuals). He then moves to see if the mother and father are in charge of the situation (hierarchy) or if their leadership is faulty.

*Example 2*

Parents obtain counseling for their teenaged son who is doing nothing constructive in school and has lost all his friends. The mother hovers around the boy continually at home, asking him what homework he has, whether he wants anything to eat, and so on. The father is a workaholic who is rarely home and is never involved with his son. The counselor sees the boundary around the mother and father (as spouses in a subunit) as weak, allowing the mother to get too close to the son. The counselor moves the parents closer together, concurrently disengaging the mother from the son and getting the father involved in the son's life.

*Example 3*

A man begins to feel more and more unfulfilled at work and at home and takes out his frustrations on his wife. The conflict gets detoured through their nine-year-old son, who is verbally attacked by both parents for various minor offenses. He begins to act up more and more at school and in the neighborhood until he comes to the attention of school authorities, who recommend counseling for him.

*Example 4*

A couple have an adolescent girl who is very withdrawn and depressed. She sits between her parents with her head down as they talk about all the pressure in their lives and in their marriage. The father is about to lose his job, and the mother is chronically depressed. It is obvious to the counselor that the parents have included the girl in too much of their personal business, violating the boundary around themselves as spouses and parents. The girl is privy to information about which she can do nothing, which feeds her sense of helplessness. The counselor marks out the boundary around the parents by asking the daughter to leave. He then tells the parents that they should not continue to share "parent information" with their daughter.

When issues that should be reserved for the parent-spouse subunit are talked about with others, there is a boundary violation. A counselor needs to excuse others in the family (even grandparents) to show to all who the parent-executives are.

Counselors sometimes encounter couples who are more than willing to discuss intimate details of their sex lives with their children. This may have come about with the more permissive, open climate in our culture. A counselor needs to move in and put a boundary around the parents as husband and wife, letting them know that such talk is inappropriate for children to hear.

*Example 5*

A single mother brings for counseling her thirteen-year-old son, who has become increasingly more belligerent with her. He will not obey any of her directives. This is not uncommon. In their book dealing with the difficulties of single-parent families, Anita Morawetz and Gillian Walker point out how typically boundaries between parent and child or between children can become blurred.[8] Sometimes the oldest child has to act as a "parent" to younger siblings. Then when the real parent moves in to assume command and discipline this "parentified child," the child balks, not wanting to return to the ranks of childhood.

## Example 6

When a single mother with two teenaged daughters talked to a counselor, it was difficult to tell if the two girls were their mother's peers, her daughters, or her "mother." In sentence after sentence the roles seemed to change. The mother had been abused by her former husband, and the girls had helped her physically and emotionally to deal with that. As a result, they had taken on responsibilities normally carried out by an adult. Now that the mother was single, she wanted to set limits with her daughters; but they were not used to being directed in this way. Also, they were not used to seeing their mother giving orders as an executive in the family. The counselor moved to clarify the roles in the family—in this case a difficult task.

## Example 7

Boundaries between generations and the hierarchy can also become blurred. A father lost his job and the mother went back to work to support the family. The grandmother was brought in to tend the children. This created a nightmare regarding who was in charge. The grandmother was ostensibly put in charge, but the father was afraid to give her much power, since he already sensed that his control was slipping away. Whenever the grandmother made a definitive move to give guidance to the children, the father countermanded her. A counselor working with this situation would have to clear up the hierarchy question: who is in control when?

## Example 8

There are many examples of grandparent troubles, in which boundaries become problematic between the generations. In one instance, a grandfather had formed an alliance with a teenaged boy against his parents. It worked like this: the parents would set strict guidelines to control their son, whose behavior was increasingly questionable. The grandfather, who lived in the same town, would criticize his son and daughter-in-law for being too harsh with the boy. He would then talk to the boy about his own sordid past when he was a teenager and how he was very hard to handle also.

Multigenerational problems such as this one can be quite knotty for a counselor to handle. First, there is the difficulty of knowing who might be involved in the situation. Then there is the problem of attempting to work with these people successfully, especially if they do not live in the community. Problems can be maintained effectively over great distances. Counselors know that grandparents can be deeply involved in family problems, even though they do not reside locally.

*Example 9*

Counselors will see siblings who fight unmercifully with each other. Sibling fighting is normal to a point, but at times it becomes vicious and needs the attention of counselors. One major problem is hierarchical in nature, when the oldest child does not receive due status for his age priority. For example, if a twelve-year-old has the same bedtime and privileges as a seven-year-old, this type of equality without regard to age spawns fighting.

Fighting can also be kindled between siblings when one is treated (usually covertly) as special by one or both parents—"the Joseph syndrome."

*Example 10*

A wife and husband are seen in counseling. The wife says to the husband, "You should just know when I need more attention." This is an example of "mind reading," a particular boundary problem where one person feels the other should automatically know his or her thoughts. Couples are particularly susceptible to this, for over time, spouses can ascertain each other's moods to a degree through nonverbal communication. This becomes unreasonable, however, when one partner expects the other to meet needs without any spoken requests.

## Change

When we speak of change, we must look at the point where the horizontal plane (time) touches the vertical (structure), for both aspects come into play. As a family moves through time, it must maintain continuity while meeting continual demands to change that come from within and without.

Living involves changing. The way families respond to change is vital. Time passes and new demands are placed on the family, creating varying amounts of stress on the family as a whole and on its individual members. How do the members and the family unit handle stress? Do they rally to help each other? Depending on how stress caused by change is handled, the family will either learn and grow or symptoms of problems will develop with one or more family members.

Families whose internal maps are too rigid with few alternative game plans, and whose boundaries to the outside world are too impassable, tend to develop problems. They attempt to apply old solutions to new situations. When they fail, they try more of the same, such as trying to spank a fifteen-year-old. When the child was five to ten years old, this worked fine. But no longer.

Change involves a coordination of members with one another. Coordination presupposes a hierarchy. Change, therefore, touches on all parts of the family structure: boundaries, hierarchy, and subsystems. The healthy family will be able to change and help each of its members adjust.

## The Healthy Family

Defining the healthy family is not easy. Because counseling tends to deal with problems, healthy families can be described only in terms of what they are not. This obscures a complete picture of the characteristics of a healthy family, yet a positive description is most valuable. To that end, there are several main points to consider in regard to the "normal" family:

Boundaries are clear and firm.

Hierarchy is well-established with a strong parental subsystem.

Spouses put each other before anyone else.

The family reaches a balance between autonomy and interdependence for its members.

The family has a large repertoire of behaviors for solving problems and negotiating life-cycle passages.

Family rules (maps) are flexible and open to change.

The family can operate in the present without being constantly haunted by the past.

Family members have a healthy involvement with others outside the family.

Communication is open, honest, and clear.[9]

## Summary

The family is assembled with a particular structure that can be seen as it carries on its business. Actually, the structure exists simultaneously with the family movement through time, giving us a comprehensive picture of family functioning from the two dimensions of time and space.

It is important to take the following questions into account in assessing family structure:

1. Who is in the various family subunits, and how are these subunits doing as they carry on their business?

2. Are boundaries around individuals, subunits, and the family as a whole clear and sufficiently operable to let information in and out without losing the identity of the particular unit?

3. Who is in charge in the family? Is it clear who directs the action?

4. As changes occur, can the family adjust as needed in such a way that it maintains its integrity and continuity?

## Notes

[1]Salvador Minuchin, *Families and Family Therapy* (Cambridge: Harvard University Press, 1974), 51.

[2]Salvador Minuchin, *Family Therapy Techniques* (Cambridge: Harvard University Press, 1982), 11ff.

[3]Minuchin, *Families and Family Therapy*, 58.

[4]Ibid., 52.

[5]A. C. Robin Skynner, *Systems of Family and Marital Psychotherapy* (New York: Brunner/Mazel, 1976), 7.

[6]Jay Haley, *Problem-Solving Therapy* (San Francisco: Jossey-Bass, 1978), 22–23.

[7]Cloe Madanes, *Strategic Family Therapy* (San Francisco: Jossey-Bass, 1981), 29–31.

[8]Anita Morawetz and Gillian Walker, *Brief Therapy With Single-Parent Families* (New York: Brunner/Mazel, 1984).

[9]Froma Walsh, *Normal Family Processes* (New York: Guilford, 1982), 26; and James L. Framo, *Explorations in Marital and Family Therapy* (New York: Springer, 1982), 199–200.

# 8
# Strategizing

Quincy looked overwhelmed as she sat in my counseling room, waiting to tell me her difficulties. She was a woman in her young thirties who had been married for seven years to a man a number of years older. In those years, she had managed to produce four children, three of whom were still in diapers. Quincy needed help. Her mother had moved in to assist, but she herself was so needy that she was more burden than relief. To compound the problems, Quincy's oldest child, a six-year-old girl, had begun to have frequent temper tantrums.

As we talked, it became apparent that Quincy's husband was not much help. He would come home and dump his own demands on her. He told her she needed to organize her time better so she could complete his agenda. He took no responsibility for the kids, for the house, or for their social life. He expected Quincy to continue to focus on him. (He fits what diagnosticians would call a classic narcissistic personality). In fact, he somewhat resented her not being more available to him. She was rapidly wearing out, and she found herself beginning to hate her kids.

I asked Quincy to relate some of her background. She had been the child of an alcoholic father and a long-suffering mother. She had learned well how to be a care-giver. She expected little from men and much from herself. She had very little sense of what a mutual relationship should look like.

Here was a case of multiple problems. Quincy had problems

115

personally. In addition, her marriage was in disarray, she was having trouble with her mother, she was not parenting effectively, and her children were showing signs of having trouble. Where should I start in my counseling? And with whom? What was the most important problem? We will examine these kinds of questions in this chapter, concentrating on effective interventions with the families who turn to counselors for help.

Remember what we have said thus far: Families, couples, and individuals have internal maps that form their unique perspective on the world. These perspectives move people to act in certain ways in the various situations of life. Our goal is to alter family, couple, and individual maps so that these people will be able to experience each other and life in general in new ways. Taking into account how the different perspectives are composed and maintained within individuals, couples, and families, we will look at strategies to alter these maps.

Counseling can be seen in two ways—either as the organizing of ideas (insight leading to individual change), or as the shaping of experience (rearrangement of relationships). If we as counselors wish to work with ideas, we will concentrate primarily on the structure of thought processes that lead to particular behaviors. The goal will be to bring about understanding, then change.

If we choose to work with relationships, we will concentrate on ongoing actions of the actors as they interact with each other. The goal will be to rearrange an interactional pattern so that people who have acted in certain ways toward each other in the past will find new ways of relating to each other. (This is not the same as behaviorism. Behaviorists don't classically work with relationships *per se.* They tend to work with the action of one person on another, not the interaction between them and others who are also involved.)

It is critical, having split the two approaches to counseling, to state that these two categories are *never* mutually exclusive. Ideas never exist in a vacuum; they are held by people who relate. Relationships are carried out and maintained by people who have certain ideas. The issue is the emphasis.

## Dimensions of the Problem

People go to counseling concerned about behaviors, thoughts, or feelings that are not as they should be. The behavior is described as deviant or distressing. The people who report this tell of unsuccessful efforts to stop or alter the behavior. They seek the counselor's help to remedy the situation. Invariably the people are demoralized. Problems start in various ways, and they can be seen from various angles. We will look at several angles.

### The Context

A counselor first decides the context within which he will work: Individual? Couple? Family? A combination of these? It is necessary to conceptualize and formulate problems in all these realms. Even more important, if a counselor is working in one realm (e.g., with an individual) and does not take into account the other realms (the person's marriage, family, family of origin), he is invariably missing valuable information.

Consider a person who seeks counseling. When a problem is seen in the context of the individual, a particular behavior or feeling is said to be troubling that person. But behavior, both normal and problematic, is continually shaped and maintained by ongoing reinforcements in that person's life. His behavior springs from his perspectives (map) on situations. But of course no one lives in a vacuum. One person's behavior instigates and shapes another person's behavior, and vice versa.

Therefore, if a person says he is depressed (an adjective from the left side), the question is what or who depresses (a verb pointing to relationship on the right side) him the most? In what contexts? When? No one stays depressed at the same level at all times with all people in all situations. Depression varies, and the counselor needs to find out who might be contributing to the situation and how.

When starting the counseling process, especially in the initial interview, it is best for us to have as many significant people present as possible. That includes spouses and children and sometimes grandmothers and grandfathers. The counselor needs to see the contexts of the person, not just listen to his perspective on what his context is.

## The Time Frame

A second issue for counselors to consider is the time frame of the problem. A counselor needs to ask, Should I work in the past, or do I concentrate on the present? Now, the histories of people can be interesting—seductively so. Hours can pass as data about "important" incidences are gathered. But the counselor must always question, Is this information important to what I'm doing with this person? A counselor should try to gather only the needed information. Many new counselors gather masses of material on a person or family, mainly because it's easy to do and nonthreatening.

But beyond this information-gathering is the question as to whether past traumas are the cause of present problems. This question could be debated endlessly. I suggest starting with the present and looking at the ongoing antecedents to the problem. If no relief can be found here, go backward. Remember, however, that patterns that continue in the present definitely have their roots in the past. For instance, if a person acts bashful with women now, it is very likely that this has been his experience most of his life. But does the counselor need to know each instance or even the beginning instance of this problem to help the person? I think not.

Many counselors agree that second-order change—the change that alters maps and transforms relationships—tends not to be the result of insight into the past. The map on the right side of the brain needs an alteration in perspective. Past experiences maintain their power and immediacy because they are still remembered on the right side as a series of motion pictures complete with all the old feelings attached.

As an example, consider a woman in her thirties who remembers being sexually abused repeatedly by her father. Having become a Christian, she knows she must forgive and prays to do so. The memories, however, maintain their power and immediacy for her as her mind relives past events with all the emotions attached. Gaining insight into these past traumas can only help so much. Because there is a continual replay of the memories in the mind, this woman needs to be guided through the old memories only from a new perspective—no longer as the abused child, but as the forgiving adult, seeing her father as Christ sees him. (This process has been carried out in a technique called "inner healing.")[1]

*Content or Relationship?*

Third, the counselor needs to decide whether to give more attention to the content of the person's communication or to the process of the relationships before him? This is not an either-or proposition. Certainly the content of the person's communication must receive attention. When a person says, "I'm depressed," the counselor needs to take this seriously and respond to it. While attending to content, the counselor needs to realize that the meaning he attaches to what the person says may not be the person's meaning.

A counselor must also look at the way people interact. Possibly this ongoing drama will give him far more valuable information than their verbalizations.

## The Position of the Counselor

Each counselor has basically one approach that he takes with all clients. This approach undoubtedly comes from the counselor's map under the heading, "What would be most helpful to people who are hurting." When the particular approach doesn't work in a given situation, the counselor tends to try more things using the same approach.

Some counselors are confrontational and immediately point out the sins and faults of everyone present. Other counselors are warm and caring, never confronting anyone. Some counselors wish to be liked by everybody, so they do everything possible to please. To a certain degree all theories of counseling methods evolve from the maps of the individual theorist. Psychoanalysts, behaviorists, humanists, family therapists, inner healers, transactional analysts, and nouthetic counselors all have unique perspectives on human behavior, and all seem to help certain people.

Each approach can be helpful in a specific situation. Sometimes, however, they do not work so well in other circumstances. Unfortunately, when the counselor finds that his approach doesn't help a particular person, he usually places the blame with the client: "He's so resistant to change." This seems a bit unfair, because the person may be merely reacting to a counselor's particular way of approaching him and the situation. If the counselor is confrontational, for example, he may remind the person of a harsh, overbearing father with whom he has had much difficulty and pain.

It is important, then, for a counselor to develop a number of different approaches. The uniqueness of each person makes a strong case for this. The counselor needs to be facile in the particular approach that could best accommodate the person who needs help. One person may need confronting; another, caring.

## What Needs to Change?

Deciding what needs to change is a crucial dimension of counseling. It is not unusual for someone to present a problem that the counselor sees as only a symptom of greater problems or knows he cannot change. Therefore a first step is for the counselor to begin to discern what his clients want to see happen and to determine if he can be helpful working with them.

The initial interview must include a mutual agreement between the counselor and a client as to what the problem is, what they are working on together, and what constitutes success. Many problems presented are so vague that the counselor would not be sure when he has seen success:

"I want to see Johnny have better self-esteem."

"I don't want to feel so depressed all the time."

"I would like to get more out of life."

"We want Mary to obey authority better."

"He needs to be more sensitive to me as his wife."

All these are classic statements about the nature of a problem. But none is framed so that the counselor can know for sure what he is working on and when he has been successful. Defining what needs to be changed has been described by one family theorist as "the thing in the bushes."[2] By this she meant that what counselors want to change will often be very elusive.

## The Time Dimension

Earlier in this book we stated that the overall goal of counseling is to work for second-order change. This change leads to altering relationships (both vertical and horizontal) accompanied by a shift in perspective (altering the map). Changing perspective has to do with a great deal more than changing a person's propositional base (his stated belief system), though this, of course, is involved. Second-order change will involve the whole way that people view themselves and others in relationship.

We have also looked at the two dimensions of the family relationship: the unfolding of the family over time, and the structure of the family at any point in time. Problems develop in families out of these two dimensions. The family has unique perspectives (the family map) on how it should be organized and should operate (the structure) at various stages of development (the time factor). When these perspectives are faulty, problems will unfold.

In chapter 6 we talked about the family moving through time, reaching various developmental plateaus that need to be successfully negotiated so the family can move to the next stage of development. At those different stages people enter or leave the family, causing varying degrees of crises. At each stage the family has to clear a particular hurdle in which each family member has to alter his perspectives of each other.

Take as an example a child's moving into adolescence. This is a precarious time when the family needs to see the child in a new way with new responsibilities. The teen is no longer a child, totally dependent on the parents. But he is also not yet a fully functioning adult. Old ways of perceiving the child must begin to fall away. Parents should be giving to the child new privileges as he rises to the occasion and accepts responsibility for newfound freedoms.

In other cases, families will seek counseling when there is mainly a developmental issue. Many of these issues arise because of faulty information. New parents do not know what to expect from their first baby. Parents of teens don't know how much freedom to give a fourteen-year-old. A retired couple has trouble coming to terms with being in each other's presence all day long.

It is important for a counselor to have a sense of what is expected at the various developmental stages so that he can act as a consultant to families. Many people need only to be reassured that what is taking place in their families is entirely normal. Consider some examples that illustrate common problems with developmental stages and how a counselor can sort through the issues.

*Example 1*

Mother and father take their oldest child, an eighteen-year-old daughter, to a counselor because they are concerned about her behavior. They state that she stays out late and insists on choosing her own clothes, friends, and activities. Now she is also breaking more of the parents' rules. The counselor learns that this girl has always been a good student and a responsible daughter, and has been generally vigilant in her demeanor.

The counselor begins to talk with the parents about adulthood and the fact that their daughter will be leaving home soon to assume a life of her own.

*Example 2*

Parents have a sixteen-year-old daughter who is basically very nice. However, they are concerned about her choice of friends and activities and the fact that she will share very little of her life with them. The initial counseling session begins to focus on the father's relationship with the girl. It seems that since she reached puberty, he has withdrawn more and more from her life even though they previously had been very close. The girl has experienced this as rejection. She is depressed about this and has responded to both parents by closing off communication with them.

The counselor points out that it is normal for fathers to feel uncomfortable with their daughters as they become women. He asks the girl whether she had ever sat on her father's lap. She says she always had until she was about twelve. The counselor asks if she would still like to. She responds, "Yes." He asks if it would be okay with the father, and he responds "Yes." The counselor instructs them to do this at least twice a week. Mother, father, and daughter are very satisfied with this intervention and never need to see the counselor again.

When a family's problem is almost totally a matter of a developmental stage, a counselor should give them information as to what should be happening. The family will usually understand what the situation is and move to make the necessary adjustments.

## Example 3

A man in his forties tells a counselor that he has to move out of his house to his own place, leaving his wife, son, daughter, and mother. He has been extremely responsible all his life, not only working a full-time job, but also running a part-time business. He has always done the right thing and rarely said no to anyone, especially his family. In fact, his life has become one of responding to the demands of others. The words "I want" have never crossed his lips. He has few friends and no personal activities that he can spend time in alone.

Now he is in the midst of "the mid-life crisis." He has all the classic symptoms. The counselor gives him a book to read that describes this time of life. He then works on getting the man to express his desires to his wife and family and to carve out pieces of time for himself. The counselor also teaches the man to say no. As a result, the man is able to stay in his marriage without the kind of radical change that is common to mid-life crises.

Many family problems, if not most, involve not only a stage of development but also the family structure. If a counselor merely gives information about the particular developmental stage and tells the family how to correct matters, nothing happens; in fact, many times the situation worsens. This cues the counselor that the problem involves not only time but also structure. The family has become stuck at this particular time because there are some faulty components in the superstructure.

Look at example 1 again. Suppose the counselor relates the appropriate expectations of a girl of this age and begins to help the family set normal guidelines of behavior—but then notices that at every turn everyone in the family is fighting him. Directives are not carried out. There is a sense that no one in the family really agrees with what the counselor says about the situation.

At this point the counselor should begin to explore more closely how the family is put together. Who is this girl close to? What role(s) in the family does she play? If she were to leave the family, how would the structure be upset? In this family at this stage, the last question is the most important. If the girl leaves home—the appropriate next step for her—would bad things begin to happen to those left behind?

*Example 4*

Consider another example of a problem that presents itself initially as simply development, but also entails structure.

A widow in her seventies is taken to a counselor by the daughter with whom she is living. The daughter is married and has several teenage children. The older woman, who has been very active and productive all her life, lapsed into depression after her husband's death and she is now unable to care for herself. At first the counselor sees this as a developmental problem; the mother needs to work through the loss of her husband, clear up any issues that still trouble her, and get on with her life.

But as the counselor works with the woman and nothing seems to improve, he explores further her living situation. He finds that the daughter and son-in-law are not getting along well and are contemplating a separation. If the mother were to get better, she could go back home to the Midwest, but then she could not help her daughter. The counselor begins to operate under the assumption that this woman has a need to stay nonfunctioning so that she can remain and keep an eye on her daughter to help where needed.

### The Space Dimension

Example 4 shows us that developmental issues that seem simple but never get resolved usually move into the realm of the family structure. Therefore a counselor should begin to systematically explore the family structure. This is analogous to a building inspector checking over the foundation and the superstructure of an edifice, peeking here and poking there to see where there might be structural problems.

There are several ways to assess the structure, and one of the best is through what Salvador Minuchin calls "enactment."[3] Instead of talking about what happened in the past, the counselor forces the action into the center of the room now. For a skilled counselor, this can be done almost from the moment the family enters the counseling room.

*Example 5*

A counselor faces a couple who are obviously angry with one another in that both have folded arms and are positioned away from each other. The counselor asks what is happening, and the wife explains that they had a fight on the way over. Remarking that it is obviously not over, the counselor suggests that the couple get back into the fight immediately to resolve it. In this way he can see how the two go about managing conflict—whether they treat each other with dignity at such times, who seems to have the most power, and so on.

As far as possible, a counselor should try to avoid intellectual discussions on what a problem is all about (including the history of the problem). It is better for him to be able to see the problem unfold in front of him, where the situation is not intellectualized, and draw his own conclusions as to what is taking place. Sometimes families are reluctant to get into such a situation; they act very proper and strenuously avoid "airing the dirty linen" except in the categories in which they wish to discuss the problem. But if the counselor will sit patiently and act bewildered, it is very likely he will eventually have an opportunity to see a full-blown argument.

Another way to check the structure of the family is to ask "and then what happened" questions. This is a technique in which the counselor asks for specific problems that the family says need to change, such as siblings fighting with each other. The counselor can have the family return to "the scene of the latest crime," so to speak, and ask step-by-step who started it, who else got involved, and how everyone achieved resolution.

*Example 6*

Consider the case of the siblings fighting. The counselor would ask the family to return in their thinking to the last time they fought. Then he would ask questions such as these:

"What started the fighting?"

"Was this the usual way, John, for you to go over and punch Bill? Or does it vary sometimes?"

"Then who got involved?"

"Mother, do you always come running when you hear the fighting?"

"How do you intercede? Whose side do you usually take?"

"Does Dad ever get involved? How? When?"

The counselor would continue to ask these kinds of questions until he has a reasonable idea how the problem usually develops and is resolved. He would be making mental notes as to who entered the fray on whose side, how the family operates, and whether this appears to be the normal pattern of relating—i.e., the family structure.

What the counselor is looking for in the structure of the family are the elements discussed in the previous chapter: subunits, boundaries, and hierarchy. Although these elements are linked and can be looked at simultaneously, let's discuss them separately for clarity.

*Subunits.* The counselor looks at the various subunits as he talks with the family—spouse, parent, sibling. Each subunit is noted for its membership (who are in it, and should they be). If inappropriate people are in the subunit, the counselor acts to remove them, as we will see later.

*Boundaries.* For some families, boundaries need to be shored up in certain areas; in others, the boundaries need to be loosened. Remember that boundaries exist around individuals, subunits, and whole families.

Initially the counselor needs to note whether or not the boundaries are clear. When an individual speaks, does he speak for himself, or does he state what others are thinking or feeling? Does each person answer the questions directed toward him, or are questions answered by another? The counselor must be very sure that each person speaks for himself. In this way he shows the family that each person is an entity unto himself with his own thoughts, feelings, gifts, abilities, etc.

Next the counselor looks at the boundaries around the various subunits. Can he determine who is in charge in the family (the executive/parental subunit)? Does this role shift, with children taking on parentlike roles? Do the husband and wife act like married people with special prerogatives for each other, or are they more loyal to one of the children (or their own parents) than to each other? If these subunits are confusing, the counselor seeks to make clear what has been lacking.

Last, the counselor notes the boundary around the whole family. Is it so rigid that the family doesn't have the benefit of information from the outside world? If so, it is probable that the family members are enmeshed in everyone else's emotional space with a great difficulty in telling who are the parents, the kids, the leaders, the followers, and so on. If this is the case, the counselor will have to work to create individuality ("I-ness") for the members of the family.

If the boundary around the whole family is too loose, there will be little loyalty among its members. Each one will be in his own orbit, and a sense of closeness and caring will be lacking. The counselor will then have to create a boundary around the family and the outside world and seek to help the family develop a sense of togetherness and cooperation.

*Hierarchy.* The counselor must determine who is in charge. If the parents are badly divided and functioning poorly as parents, he needs to start work there. First he should put the mother and father together physically in the room by moving any children sitting between them. This at least shows visually to everyone that the two are together. Then the counselor should address the couple as a unit and have them talk about what has made it hard in the past to agree and pull together.

*Example 7*

A mother and father seek counseling for a nine-year-old boy who is totally out of control at home (though he is somewhat in control with outsiders). The boy will kick and scream, especially at his mother. He will not go to church or other places the family wants to go. He is abusive with his younger sister, and his mother is afraid of him physically.

As the counselor talks with the couple, he discovers that the father tends to be peripheral to the situation. He lets his wife do most of the disciplining. He will enter in occasionally to help, but his measures are uneven and inconsistent and—according to the mother—occasionally too harsh. After seeing the whole family once, the counselor has the mother and father come in alone (to set a boundary around them as executives) and begins to work with them to come to agreement. The mother wants techniques of discipline, but the counselor gives her none. He always directs her to her husband to work out guidelines and disciplinary consequences for the boy.

In working with couples who cannot control their children,

we will find that they often tend to discount each other and undercut whatever measures the other initiates. If the counselor cannot get consensus from the parents to work together, there is little use in giving guidelines for exercising discipline—the couple will not effectively administer them. Rarely do parents lack specific skills in parenting; more often than not they know how to parent, but they just have not been able to be mutually supportive and in agreement as to how to get the job done.

A counselor needs to determine whether the lines of authority in a family are clear and whether everyone abides by these lines. When the parents can't control the family, many times it is very likely that someone outside the immediate family—usually a grandparent—is cutting the lines of authority.

*Example 8*

A couple have a five-year-old son whom they simply cannot control. The boy will do what he pleases even though ostensibly the parents seem to be of one mind as to what they want for him. Jay Haley has said that a child cannot gain control of a family without standing on the shoulders of someone else.[4] In this case, the mother's mother is the culprit. She will periodically enter the family and criticize her daughter's parenting while giving tacit endorsement to the child's misdeeds.

The counselor's task is to work out with the parents a way of removing the grandmother from the situation so that they can regain control. This seems herculean, since it is difficult to honor grandparents as individuals in God's order while simultaneously removing them from the family.

Being clear about the parenting subunit is related to the need to be clear about the spouse subunit. Parents who chronically disagree tend to be a couple who lack intimacy. They do not spend quality time alone together, and this is one big reason why they get into trouble as they attempt to be executives. If they can get and keep a healthy, intimate relationship going smoothly, they can usually come together to direct the raising of the children in a suitable fashion. As a counselor works with a family, he should try to discover whether the parents ever spend time alone together just doing things they like to do.

Married couples who do not get along tend to be persons who

have become locked into one or two issues that dominate their relationship. If a counselor sees that the spouses aren't getting along, he must be very careful not to recommend too quickly that the marriage needs work, especially when the agenda for seeking counseling is someone else or something other than the marriage. If he confronts the marital issues too quickly when they want something else changed, the couple will tend to resist strongly and will not go along with his observations. Their response could sound something like this:

> "No, you have it all wrong. It's not our marriage that needs help; we get along just fine. It's our son who is the problem. You must help him to quit acting up."

If a couple seeks counseling specifically for marital work, or if they are at a point where they will agree that their marriage needs attention, then the counselor can work with them to find the recursive patterns that dominate the relationship. "Recursive" means that couples will go round and round on the same issues in virtually the same ways because they are deadlocked and cannot find the way out. The issue is not better communication, although communication invariably has deteriorated. The couple see and treat each other in ways that have become rigid and unhelpful. As time has passed, the patterns have solidified and the couple have trouble changing perspective.

> "He's always so thoughtless."
>
> "She will never go along with my suggestions."
>
> "All he thinks about is himself."
>
> "She's just mean and nasty all the time."

The use of superlatives is often a giveaway that a person is seeing the spouse in a one-dimensional, troubled way that has distorted all the other characteristics of the spouse. Usually this distortion also involves a boundary violation: I have trouble accepting a certain trait in me, and as a result I attribute that trait to my partner. Here are some examples:

> I have trouble dealing with anger. I provoke anger in my partner and see her as an angry person.

I am concerned about my skills as a parent. Whenever I deal with the children, I feel my spouse's disapproval.

I have difficulty with emotional closeness. As my partner attempts to get close, I pull away, which makes her feel rejected.

I have trouble with my self-esteem. I provoke my partner to the point that he is constantly critical of me, lowering my sense of esteem.

These pieces, as we said earlier, are parts of the individual map that are still unresolved and intense. In marriage, a person attempts unconsciously to work through these issues with the spouse. Of course, it is never realized or announced that the issue is being worked through. These pieces of unfinished business have a way of surfacing on their own, precisely because they are unfinished and need to be settled.

When the spouse is also unresolved and intense about the same issue, there is usually a mutual inability to work through the issue, mainly because neither spouse can find the proper distance from it to work effectively. If a person has trouble dealing with anger but marries someone who can handle this adequately, his partner would be able to shepherd him through this issue. But if both spouses have difficulty with anger, they have the ingredients to set up a cyclical pattern around the issue, neither of them able to help the other resolve it.

When dealing with couples, the counselor must recognize where these intense issues are and then help the pair deal with them constructively so that they can get out of the rut and get on with other issues. The counselor notes the structure of the family and the developmental stage to see what might be amiss. At the same time, he is listening to the family describe their perspectives on the problem. Each person's perspective or frame on the problem may need changing, or reframing.

## Reframing

As the experiences of life crash in on a person and his family, the members take out their individual and collective maps to try to bring meaning to all that transpires. Maps bring focus. Focus is a narrowing process that involves straining out certain factors while highlighting others to give them particular meaning. These highlighted features in any situation are what we have called the person's unique perspective.

Virtually every experience we have is seen from our unique perspective. We don't notice that this process occurs constantly. It continues automatically as we attach meaning to all that we see.

People in counseling view a situation from a particular perspective. They frame the situation and the people involved in it according to this subjective viewpoint. They report certain facts to the counselor: "He . . . did this . . . at this time. . . ." But these facts are arranged and punctuated in certain ways that give a particular slant to the situation. Acts are seen with meaning. Interpretations are given. Motives are supplied. The slant sounds something like this: "He (who is basically a cad) . . . did this (reprehensible act) . . . at the (worst possible) time (for me)."

We do not label our interpretations and meanings. We just throw them in as part of the narrative, assuming that any intelligent person will come to the same conclusions given the merits of the case. This, of course, is obviously the way our maps work. They work unconsciously (right brain) and automatically and are rarely open to scrutiny.

| The Fact | The Frame |
|---|---|
| He is sick! | Isn't it awful! |
| She disobeyed. | She is a bad girl. |
| He ignored me. | He is insensitive. |
| She tells jokes. | She is a funny girl. |
| He spoke harshly. | He is a tyrant. |
| She thinks a lot. | She is obsessive. |
| He has body odor. | He is socially unacceptable. |

Of all the strategies that can be used to bring about change, the one that is probably the most important is reframing. If our goal is to change perspective, to alter the map, to rearrange the relationship, the perceptual framework of the situation must be changed. This process of change we call "reframing."

As people place meaning and value on things and experiences, they force objects and events into classes from which it is hard to escape. All behavior has numerous strains of motivation.

132                                                    Counseling Families

All motives are contaminated as a result of mankind's fall into sin.
As people look at the facts of certain situations, it becomes all too
easy to pick up the negative, contaminated strains of the
motivation:

> "She does that only because she seeks attention."
>
> "He's power hungry; of course he acts that way."
>
> "If he really liked you, he would act differently."

A family in trouble is usually a family that is framing one
member as "sick" or a "problem" because of certain actions that
have been observed. Other factors have been strained out and
ignored as the frame has become more rigid over time. Individuals
who seek help from a counselor have also narrowed their focus to
take in only certain factors, which are the irregular ones. Assets,
benefits, gifts, and talents are usually forgotten or minimized; this
is especially true for people who are depressed, but it holds to a
degree for everyone who seeks help.

The family invariably ignores its own structure—its boundaries, hierarchy, and subsystem functioning. It also tends to
discount where it is in its passage through time. What has taken
the focus is *this problem* seen in *this individual,* period! And it is
always assumed that the way that the behavior is framed (i.e., as a
particular problem) is the only frame that can possibly apply.

The frame is like a tinted pair of glasses. It colors all that it
observes. People in a family respond to individuals according to the
frame. Once a person is seen and framed as the funny man in a
family, he can read the phone book and people will be in tears
laughing.

Only the troubling frames end up in the counselor's office.
And it is the counselor's job to attach new meaning to situations
that have become problematic and hopeless.

The idea of reframing emerges powerfully in Scripture. As we
become Christians, our situations don't necessarily change, but our
perspectives of them—the frames—do. Christians don't sit idly by
in the grip of circumstances. Even in the bad (frame) circumstances we see God at work.

Reframing is not foolish whistling in the dark, calling bad

good. If that were the case, reframing would never work, because the right side of the brain would "see" right through the mirage.

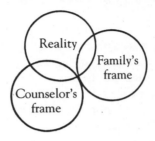

Figure 8.1: **Reframing**

A counselor needs to take two important steps while reframing a client's perception of a problem. The first step is to understand the particular frame being used by the family. The family will call some behavior deviant or problematic. A particular problem is seen a particular way. It is important to see how each family member frames the problem. It is also important to hear the particular language that each member uses and the specific images and metaphors used to frame the problem. These images will be helpful later when the new frame is constructed.

As an example, a couple has a nineteen-year-old son. The father calls the son "irresponsible"; the mother calls him "sick." The parents have observed the same behavior, but they have established different frames.

Another example is a husband who complains that his wife nags him all the time, never noticing how his own passivity at home activates his wife to peck at him.

Consider also a wife who becomes overly concerned when her husband gains five pounds—which are not even noticeable to his friends—and fears (and frames) that he is "letting himself go."

It is helpful to understand where these particular frames come from. As we have seen, people are constantly framing the behavior of all members of their family. This is a universal truth. And certain behaviors are marked out as different, sick, or abnormal, according to the intense, unresolved issues in a person's map. Families are a convenient place for these issues to be projected onto others; we see conflicted areas in ourselves acted out in the lives of those closest to us. Our loved ones act in ways that are familiar and difficult to us; we cannot see these acts objectively and dispassionately.

It is not imperative initially for us as counselors to know the whole process of how the frames developed. The important first step is to see what the frames are and to what behavior they refer. After we have discerned the frames, we immediately move to put the problem into a new, relational frame.

As mentioned, the frames brought by clients tend not to be particularly workable for the counselor. There are two reasons for this: (1) the terms used are vague ("depressed," "hyperactive," "obsessive," "unspiritual," "rebellious"), and (2) the frames presented are in individual categories ("He's the only one who is sick here").

A counselor should look for the operation of the couple or the whole family to see how the behaviors suggested are played out in the context. From this observation he will develop the new frame for the problem and present it to the family for approval. Consider some examples:

| Family Frame | Counselor's Reframing |
|---|---|
| He's a perfectionist. | Nothing he does will satisfy his family. |
| She's a juvenile delinquent. | She will pay no attention to you at all. |
| He's depressed. | He doesn't know his place in the family, and he doesn't feel important. |
| She's uncontrollable. | She never thinks you mean it when you tell her what to do. |
| He's abusive. | He feels so inadequate with you that he feels he has only his fists to gain parity. |
| She's frigid. | For some reason she doesn't respond to you sexually. |
| He's a nag. | Somehow he's become your conscience. |
| She fights with mother. | She's trying to teach father how to fight with mother. |

A counselor cannot continue until all members of a family are able to accept his new frame in place of their own. If he makes one of these statements, he must be able to observe nonverbally or hear verbally that all agree that his reframing is the correct frame from which to work.

If the counselor finds that he absolutely cannot persuade the family to accept his frame, he reassesses his reasoning to see if he might have considered the problem wrongly. If so, he forms another frame for the family. In some instances he may feel certain that his reframing is correct, but the family is not yet ready to accept a new frame that includes relationships. It is said, "If you can change what the experience means to them, their response will change."[5] Establishing a relational frame has the quality of shifting perspective to a degree. The family is made to see the problem from a relational point of view: "You have a problem . . . with her." The problem is no longer residing just with the individual.

The new frame is also delivered to set in motion the changes in the individual and family maps. Remember, as the reframing is delivered, the facts of the situation do not change, only the meaning that is attached to the facts. As the meaning is changed, the emotional consequences for the family will also change. As these emotional consequences change, the family members' ways of behaving vis-à-vis the problem will change.

Again, it should be emphasized that we are *not* trying to say "bad" is "good" or put some esoteric interpretation on a situation. We as counselors attach a meaning to the facts that is as valid as the family interpretation, but is heretofore unnoticed or ignored. In doing this we focus attention on another aspect of the situation or onto another person.

A good reframing must take into account all the family members and how they interrelate in ways that perpetuate the problem at hand.

Reframing in effect sets the stage for all our subsequent maneuvers. It places the problem in a context previously ignored by the family from which we can work most thoroughly. It also has the quality of changing the perspectives (maps) of the family, to see old problems in new, more hopeful ways. Experienced counselors tend to reframe almost unconsciously as families present their problems. Counselors immediately draw tentative hypotheses as to what is happening and reframe the problems according to their appraisal. If the reframing is rejected, the counselors work to see whether they have analyzed the situation wrongly or the family is not yet ready to accept the reframe.

As an exercise, try listing on paper the family problems that you have heard of in the past—problems that may or may not end up in a counselor's office. Beside each problem suggest some possible alternative perspectives on what the problem might mean. List some examples given in this book if you wish. It is important to see that problems can have many windows and explanations; a counselor's job is to test these alternatives.

Reframing, then, is used in conjunction with the family structure and the stages of a family's development. Both dimensions are necessary for the family to take into account as they consider their problem.

Suppose a family seeks counseling for a daughter they frame as uncontrollable. In his reframing, the counselor explains how facets of the hierarchy structure are not functioning properly: "Mom and Dad, she never thinks you mean it when you tell her to do something. Why is that?" Notice that in this reframing he calls into question the executive subsystem and the hierarchy. If a child is not obeying, there is usually a problem in these parts of the structure, and his reframing reflects this truth.

In another example, parents have a nineteen-year-old boy who is framed as depressed. To work with this frame is to accept the idea that the seat of the problem resides in the boy and that it is his problem *alone*. On further examination the counselor finds that the boy had been away at college when he learned of tension between his parents back home. He became "depressed," dropped out of school, and returned home. The counselor's reframing must take into account the developmental stage (young person leaving home) and the structure (mother and father not getting along, boy important to "referee" their relationship). His reframing is, "It's difficult for you to get on with your life when you're not sure mother and father can make it on their own."

A typical complaint is an adolescent who fights with a parent. This is normal to a point, but when it ends up in a counselor's office, more is usually involved. The frame of the parents might be, "Mary fights with her mother all the time." This sounds like a proper frame, for it takes into account a relationship (mother and sixteen-year-old Mary). But on further examination, the counselor finds that the father is weak and never confronts his wife, thus letting her dominate the family. The reframing might well be that Mary is trying to teach father how to fight mother. It is true that when a child fights frequently with a parent, he may be unconsciously fighting for the other parent.

Here are several other reframings that a counselor can use:

- A husband who comes home and fights with his wife and children or withdraws into the den by himself. Our new frame is this: *You've lost your place in your family. How can we get it back?*
- A boy who never remembers his schoolwork and is nagged constantly by his mother. Our frame is as follows: *Mother has taken your mind and does your thinking for you. How can we help you get your mind back?*
- A teenaged girl who acts totally irresponsibly in her life while her parents—especially dad—bails her out of every difficulty. Our frame: *Dad is subsidizing her irresponsibility.*
- A wife who refuses to bring up tough issues with her husband. Our frame: *You treat him as if he's fragile. Will he really break if you share these things with him?*
- A husband and father who is marginal in the family. Our frame is, *You never seem to make a difference with your family, and as a result, you don't know where you fit in.*

## Summary

To assess what needs to change and the way to go about moving the family in the direction of change, the counselor should incorporate the following:

1. Assess the family structure to see what elements need to be corrected, strengthened, or eliminated.

2. Note where the family is developmentally and, if an assist with a troubling developmental task is in order, make the necessary adjustments.

3. Construct a new frame to focus the family attention on the problem so that a new perception can be gained.

## Notes

[1] The concept of "inner healing" has been developed in a number of books, including Michael Scanlan, *Inner Healing* (New York: Paulist,

1974); Leanne Payne, The Broken Image (Westchester, N.Y.: Corner-stone, 1978); and David Seamands, The Healing of Memories (Wheaton, Ill.: Victor, 1985).

   [2]Lynn Hoffman, Foundations of Family Therapy (New York: Basic, 1981), 176.

   [3]Salvador Minuchin, Family Therapy Techniques (Cambridge: Harvard University Press, 1981), 78ff.

   [4]Jay Haley, Problem-Solving Therapy (San Francisco: Jossey-Bass, 1976), 100ff.

   [5]Richard Bandler and John Grinder, Reframing: Neuro-Linguistic Programming and the Transformation of Meaning (Moab, Utah: Real People, 1982), 7.

# 9
# Synthesizing

Now two prostitutes came to the king and stood before him. One of them said, "My lord, this woman and I live in the same house. I had a baby while she was there with me. The third day after my child was born, this woman also had a baby. We were alone; there was no one in the house but the two of us.

"During the night this woman's son died because she lay on him. So she got up in the middle of the night and took my son from my side while I your servant was asleep. She put him by her breast and put her dead son by my breast. The next morning, I got up to nurse my son—and he was dead! But when I looked at him closely in the morning light, I saw that it wasn't the son I had borne."

The other woman said, "No! The living one is my son; the dead one is yours."

But the first one insisted, "No! The dead one is yours; the living one is mine." And so they argued before the king.

The king said, "This one says, 'My son is alive and your son is dead,' while that one says, 'No! Your son is dead and mine is alive.'"

Then the king said, "Bring me a sword." So they brought a sword for the king. He then gave an order: "Cut the living child in two and give half to one and half to the other."

The woman whose son was alive was filled with compassion for her son and said to the king, "Please, my lord, give her the living baby! Don't kill him!'

But the other said, "Neither I nor you shall have him. Cut him in two!"

Then the king gave his ruling: "Give the living baby to the first woman. Do not kill him; she is his mother" (1 Kings 3:16–27).

This story about King Solomon represents one of the most dramatically successful interventions by a counselor ever recorded. With a simple yet profound action he was able to ascertain the truth and make the proper prescription.

Today's counselors have similar tasks. They must hear and observe the problems people bring to them. They must assimilate the data to discern reality. Then they must provide an arena for meaningful change.

To accomplish these goals, the counselor has to work hard. A wrong turn can be taken at any stage of the counseling process. Let us examine that process to enable it to have the greatest effect possible for problem-solving.

### Setting the Stage

Phones ring on counselors' desks all over the country every day. That initial contact of receiving a telephone call is crucial to the counseling that follows.

A counselor should attend to phone calls with great care, remembering that this makes the caller's first impression. Immediate judgments are made as to the counselor's competence and attentiveness. The stage is also set for the rest of counseling, for in a real sense, the initial contract for counseling is established on the phone. Many people testify that they have selected or rejected counselors merely because of the way they were treated in a phone call. A counselor can learn from this.

First, a counselor must immediately let people know when they call that he is sympathetic to their distresses but is also the person in charge of the counseling. It always amazes me how many people call me (implying that I am some sort of expert in human relations) and then try to debate with me how the counseling will proceed. As the years have passed, I have become more adamant with callers as to the arrangements I expect.

Second, a counselor should tell the caller that he wants *everyone* involved in the problem to be present for the first interview. The caller will think that the only one involved is the person who is showing the symptoms or problems. It must be made clear that if the problem involves a child or young adult living at home, the counselor needs to see everyone in the immediate family. If the issues are marital, he will want to see both partners in the first session.

It is often at this point that the protests begin. People say that so-and-so won't come or will be uncomfortable coming—which usually means the *caller* will be uncomfortable. The counselor should say something like "I'm sorry, but I can't be effective unless I see everyone."

When the situation involves a child who is out of control in a divorced, single-parent situation, the counselor will usually want to see the ex-spouse also. At this point, however, he should make allowances for the fact that there might be a great deal of hostility standing between the divorced couple. If the former spouse won't attend, the counselor must be particularly careful during the first interview to try to determine if he can really help effect change without having both parents involved in the counseling.

Counseling can quickly get out of control if the counselor relinquishes some of his standards in an attempt to accommodate. One potentially disastrous consequence entails coalitions. Invariably as counseling begins, each person involved in the problem would like the counselor's sympathies. But if only certain people are present initially, only these perspectives will be given. It is very difficult to involve others in subsequent sessions if they are not present at the outset, probably because people feel that someone who was there first will have swayed the counselor's mind.

A counselor must be careful not to form a coalition with the person making the initial call. When people call, the counselor should ask them for a short synopsis of the problem so that he can state whom he would like to have attend the first interview. Most callers want to go on and on about their particular perspective on a problem, especially when they disagree with the request to have other people present. The counselor can politely tell them that he needs only a short summary and that he will get the details when they all sit down together. One counselor said he finds it helpful to say, "I have difficulty digesting complex information on the phone. May I suggest we discuss it further at the appointment time?"[1]

Sometimes a caller will request a specific form of counseling, such as individual, inner healing, or hypnosis. After telling the caller what he normally does and does not do, the counselor can say that he must see the nature of the problem before he can recommend what particular approach to use. Generally the counselor would also like to know why the caller feels the particular approach mentioned would be effective for him.

A counselor should not hesitate to state his credentials over the phone, including his schooling, training, and experience. If people know he is a Christian, they may ask about particular spiritual experiences also: "Are you Spirit-filled?" Each counselor will have to decide for himself where to draw the line on discussing particular beliefs. It is important to realize that behind these questions is a desire to know that the counselor can be trusted; therefore many counselors do not see these questions as intrusive.

Initially the counselor needs to establish the hour for the first session and how long it will last. This could be especially important for ministers or other counselors who do not schedule their office hours the same way as other professional counselors. People tend to think that a minister's schedule is very flexible and that he should always be at the disposal of the congregation. To set clear limits and be able to say no firmly is crucial.

Many phone calls involve requests for counseling for a third party. An experienced counselor said, "I entertain such requests when it is the parent of a child who is calling, or if one spouse is calling for both for marital work. If someone calls and asks for an appointment for a friend, or if a parent requests an appointment for an adult child, I ask that the person in question call me directly."[2]

Invariably, when a person calls to request counseling for an adult child or friend, that subject is dependent on the caller in some way and has given responsibility for significant parts of his life over to the caller. I like adults to take responsibility for their own lives, starting with calling me for an appointment.

Now we come to the issue of whom to see in counseling. A beneficial general policy is to include everyone who is involved in the problem in the first session when this is physically possible. Remembering that it is much harder to persuade people to come after the first session, the counselor should try to assess during the phone call whom he needs and then request their presence.

After the initial session the counselor may discover that he will have to cast a broader net to bring in more people. For example, a man went to a counselor with acute anxiety attacks. After working with the anxiety to no avail, the counselor asked the wife to come also. It appeared as though she cared for him almost too much, but it was discovered that all their parents lived just a block away and "overnurtured" him. Eventually the counselor had both his parents and hers in for counseling.

If a family comes in stating that one member refused to come, the counselor should consider calling that member to tell him how important his perspective on the situation is, that he has data that no one else in the family understands.

In divorce and single-parent situations, letters can be written to noncustodial parents to urge them to come and help plan a coherent plan for their children. An illustration is this letter a counselor wrote to the father of two small children, who had separated from his wife and would not come in for counseling:

> It seems clear to me that the children are deeply attached to you and you to them. Furthermore, I have the sense that there are many areas in your children's lives that you understand better than your wife. There are important areas that would be particularly helpful to your children.[3]

The same counselor was once seeing a family about control of their sixteen-year-old son, who was having a behavior problem at school. The boy decided one week not to come to the session. The counselor had already ascertained that the boy was masking conflict between his parents, so he wrote him this:

> I want to congratulate you on your bold move of not showing up for the family session today. By this decisive stroke you have managed to keep the focus on yourself. I know that there are many tensions in your family, tensions that could cause a lot of hurt if they were to surface. With the focus squarely on you, I feel confident that this tension will never land on anyone else and be allowed to hurt them. Keep up the good work. As long as you hold out, your father, mother, and sister will never have to feel the pain.[4]

The young man showed up for the session the next week.

As for the particular place to hold sessions, a comfortable, simple room is highly desirable. One counselor uses identical chairs, placed in a circle. He never sits behind a desk. He waits for the family to find a place ("Anywhere is fine") and then takes whatever seat is left. From the outset he stresses confidentiality: "The things said in this room should stay here."

We should be aware that ministers are far more likely to breach confidentiality than other counselors, even though clergy privilege is most sacred under common law. So a minister may have to be even more clear and forceful regarding the need for total confidentiality.

## The Initial Interview

I always have two critical questions in mind whenever anyone calls me, and when I finally have them come in to see me: "What is the problem here?" and "Can I be of help in this situation?" Probably the most powerful statement I learned in counseling was "I'm sorry, I'm not the one to help you." Unfortunately, the counseling field is full of folks who feel omnipotent (I know, I used to be one of them) who take on all problems at all times. After a while they usually begin to feel totally overwhelmed and ineffective, and then burn out.

A woman brought to me her ten-year-old son who is totally out of control at school and at home. She is a single mother with few financial resources and virtually no family left in the country who can be of any emotional or financial help to her. She has seen several counselors and two ministers at her church (who referred her to me). She is a combination of anger and depression and clutches at counselors like a drowning man clutches the lifeguard.

She looked at me incredulously as I told her I would *only* help her with setting proper boundaries for her son. I told her that I could not handle all of the other problems, that I would call her minister and discuss with him how the other concerns could be managed within the church community. She had enormous expectations of me, and I knew I would soon be smothered under a mountain of problems if I didn't set limits quickly and clearly.

### The Aim

As the family gathers for the initial interview, the counselor needs to assemble adequate information on basic matters:

1. What is the nature of the complaint?
2. How is the problem being handled?
3. What are the minimal goals of everyone present?
4. What is everyone's position in the family vis-à-vis everyone else? Who is doing what that presents a problem, to whom, and how does that present a problem?

## The Expectations

Next the counselor needs to know what the family expects of him. Some expectations will be voiced directly. Others, the counselor knows, are there but he needn't ask about them right away. Several expectations bear special caution.

First is the notion that the counselor is the expert: the family will tell him the problem and he will fix it. This plays directly into his "omnipotence" and therefore can be very seductive. It's already very flattering that people have sought out his advice in the first place.

If this expectation is held, the family will usually see themselves as passive recipients of the counselor's wisdom. The thought of taking charge themselves and actively entering into the change process has not occurred to them.

It is good to approach all families and couples from a "one-down" position, the opposite of the "one-up" and "expert" position. The counselor should never attempt to put forward an attitude of superiority. Rather, he should come across as a humble seeker who will walk along with the family as they attempt to negotiate through the labyrinth of their difficulties. When people attempt to solicit quick answers and advice, he can become "perplexed" and scratch his head.

This may sound as though it contradicts what we said earlier about being in charge of the counseling. Actually there is a bit of a paradox here, for within the boundaries of how he will conduct counseling—which must be rigidly maintained—he should be humble about the change process and the way all of them will move toward it.

This is not to say that the counselor doesn't have a plan as to where he wants to go. Usually he will know to a degree what he is looking for on the basis of his basic information about the family. He can never be absolutely sure where his observations and questions may lead him, however. In particular, he never wants the family to think that he has taken over their responsibility or that his "infinite" wisdom will take charge of the situation and point the way.

Understandably, some families would love for the counselor to take charge, be the expert, come on strong, and give lots of advice quickly. Then when things go poorly and fail, the family can lay the blame with the counselor. It is preferable for him not to commit too quickly to any answer or course of action until he is fairly sure he has a proper perspective on the situation. Of course, in working with relationships and the complexities we have already discussed, care and patience are necessary to ascertain all that is happening in a given situation.

Another expectation of family members is that they will only be involved minimally in the counseling: "After all, it's Junior who has the problem." At this point there is a danger that the counselor will blame the parents, accusing them of hurting their children, especially as faulty patterns of child-rearing emerge. The hope is that they will listen, see their own culpability, and begin to make serious changes.

But actually this type of statement—"you're to blame"—will only lead to a battle as to who is at fault, and it's a battle the counselor can never win. His job is not to lay blame, but to bring about change. He should respond that everyone is important to him and he is ineffective without total involvement from all members: "Yes, I can see that Junior has a problem, but I know from experience that each of you here will be of invaluable assistance to me as I seek to help."

Many people, including Christians, think that counseling is always a long process where people come individually to counselors for a long time until insights into the truth emerge. The fact that the counselor is going to work with all family members to help bring about change may come as a surprise, although more and more people today have heard of "family counseling." If the approach is explained adequately and people know that the goal is not to take sides and place blame, families tend to go along with the proceedings willingly.

## The Position of the Client

Each person who appears in a counselor's office, whether he is identified as the problem person or just a concerned family member, has a perspective on the nature and origin of the problem. Remember all that we have said about perspective. Each person has his particular outlook on reality. Unfortunately, we tend not to realize that our perspective is unique to us and is not absolute truth.

Usually one person in the family is defined as the one with the problem—the identified patient. Most families also have a good idea as to how the problem should be resolved. It is crucial to have family members delineate the nature of the problem.[5] The counselor must listen carefully to hear how the person identified as the patient is defined. Some will define him as being "sick." If this is the case, he is understood not to be responsible for or in control of his actions. He may also be seen as the victim of someone who is "bad."

The identified patient may also be defined as being "bad." In such a case he is seen to be responsible for and in control of his actions.

As the counselor hears "the problem person" defined as sick or bad, it is important that he not initially take a particular stand. Frequently family members hold different views of the person. A typical scenario is a mother who sees her son as sick and in need of therapy, while the father defines the same boy as bad and in need of stricter discipline.

The counselor wants to know not only how the identified patient—sometimes referred to as "the symptom bearer"—is viewed, but also how the situation is perceived. Some family members will see the situation as very pressing and painful. The problems are reaching a crescendo, and help is desperately needed. The people who hold this position are the best motivated for counseling. Others will see the situation as uncomfortable, but not particularly urgent. Such a case immediately begins to cast doubt as to whether counseling is indicated at this time. The counselor looks for people who really want to change. If their motivation is low, the counselor may choose to excuse himself from helping until such time as the motivation is higher, even if the symptoms seem intolerable. In such situations there is nothing worse than a counselor who has a great deal of energy about a problem trying to rally a family with low motivation.

Along this line, it is also helpful to see who in the family is optimistic about solving the problem and who is pessimistic. Then the counselor can find out why there is a difference in attitude.

### Getting Started With the Family

The trick of all relationship interviewing is to gather information in two different arenas at the same time: the content arena and the process arena. This is one place where the skill of counseling becomes apparent. To attend to one to the neglect of the other is to miss vital information. First, consider some questions about the content of the problem. These questions should keep the family from just rambling along about needless details.

What brings you here *at this time?*

When does the symptom happen? How? Where? With whom?

What is each family member doing when the symptom happens?

How does it go away?

Who is upset by the problem? Worried? Sad? Angry? Embarrassed?

Who in the family has had similar problems?

What does each family member do at work and school? Are they doing okay? Do they have any special circumstances? Concerns? Worries?

What would change if the problem went away?[6]

As he is asking the content questions, the counselor is also assessing the process of the family. The process information can essentially be gathered in two ways. In the first method, the counselor observes the process of the family enacted. In other words, instead of asking a family how they carry on their business, he asks them to carry it on right in front of him. Some examples will illustrate how this works.

*Example 1*

A mother and father have a four-year-old daughter whom they describe as unruly. They proceed to go into intricate detail with the counselor about all her mischief. The child becomes restless in the session. The counselor asks the parents to control her.

## Example 2

A family enters the counselor's office for the first time. To begin the session, the counselor asks all family members various questions about their lives. The mother cuts everyone off and answers the questions for them. The counselor turns to the father and says, "Does your wife always answer everyone's questions like this?"

## Example 3

A mother bitterly complains that her husband is never involved with his son. The counselor turns to the father and tells him to come sit by his son and talk to him about his school work. The counselor observes how everyone reacts to this directive.

## Example 4

The counselor asks the husband to take his wife's hand and tell her about the struggles he has had that day. The counselor observes how the wife responds to the situation.

The second method for gathering process information about a family is by asking circular questions in which a family member is asked to comment on the relationship between two other family members. This is rarely done in normal family situations, and the effects can be profound. Here are some possible queries:

Is mother closer to Bill or to Mary?

Who gets more upset, mother or father? Who is the tougher?

Five years from now, who will be closest to father?

Was father closer to Sarah when she was a little girl than now?

If instead of father always leaving, mother left, what would happen?

When father and son are fighting, what does mother do?

The point is to see how problems function in a family. These are questions that deal with relationship, that part of the situation that is rarely attended to. The questions may seem strange to the family, but the information will be most helpful in determining how problems germinate and grow.

As he gathers information about the family, the counselor forms hypotheses as to what is going on. These hypotheses are tested through more observation and discussion until a proper understanding of the situation is achieved.

Gathering this kind of information is like climbing a mountain. The climbers begin to trek along a path that will apparently lead to the summit. However, the path may lead to a dead end, forcing the climbers to abandon that path and seek an alternate route. Remember that relationships are complex. Understanding how they work requires a great deal of patience and persistence.

### The Phases of the Interview

The counseling session can be arbitrarily divided into three stages: the social, the problem formulation, and the resolution. Consider how each of these works.

During the social stage the family is presumably made to feel welcome and comfortable in the counselor's office. Actually the counselor can start this stage in the waiting area when he first meets the family.

It is very important that every member of the family is greeted by the counselor. Each person must know that he is important to the ongoing process of counseling. The counselor should also ask at least one question of everyone.

"How was your day?"

"What's been happening in school?"

"What important things have you done today?"

Although none of the questions has to do with counseling per se, this stage can provide valuable information on the family's organization and functions. This stage seems innocuous, so the family tends not to be guarded. Therefore interaction is fairly natural and easygoing.

The counselor may choose to swing immediately into a full-scale discussion of the family's ways of dealing with each other based on simple things that have happened during the social stage.

151

As the family is seated, the counselor can begin to make tentative hypotheses on how this family is organized. Remember, there are two arenas that demand attention: the content and the process. Hypothesizing is an exercise that continues throughout counseling. The counselor should constantly ask himself, "What is going on here?" and the related question, "What do I need to do about it?"

When the social stage is over—usually in about five minutes—the counselor might say something like, "It's time to get down to business." This draws a distinct boundary to let the family know that he has moved into the next level of the interview: the problem-formulation stage.

Now the counselor wants to know what is going on in this family that brings them into counseling. He can start by asking children present if they know who he is and what the group are going to do today. He wants to know what they have been told by parents and something of what they expect to happen. He can then tell everyone what he has been told on the phone by the initial caller.

Let me issue a warning at this point. Many times callers, when they discover that the initial session will involve everyone, will attempt to tell the counselor things "in confidence" that they do not wish to be brought up in the session with everyone else—the fact that dad is an alcoholic, Mom had a child out of wedlock, Junior is "strung out" on drugs. Whenever anyone attempts to tell him a secret, he should realize they are in fact trying to enter into a coalition with him against other family members, a circumstance that would undoubtedly prove destructive in the long run.

When the counselor knows at any time—after sessions, when one member hangs back, is an opportune time for this to happen— that someone is trying to give him "privileged" information, he should tell the person that he would rather not hear it privately, that he doesn't know what to do with such information, and that he would feel more comfortable to have it brought up for everyone to work on.

As the problem-formulation stage unfolds, the counselor's goal is to induce everyone to give him a perspective on what is wrong. It is absolutely essential in this stage to elicit *workable* problems. Almost without exception, problems are presented in a form that is totally incomprehensible and unworkable:

"He's depressed."

"She's disobedient."

"He won't communicate with me."

"She has a poor self-image."

All these categories point to what we said earlier about the imitation of words to express experience. The examples give an idea as to what is being felt, but these categories need a great deal of expansion. The temptation is for the counselor to read his own experience into these words and to assume that there is consensus as to the problem expressed.

Using the questions we have listed previously, we can begin to dissemble these problems to find out what they mean. Take, for instance, the statement "He's depressed." First the counselor can turn to the designated person and make him answer for himself, "Is that true? Are you depressed?"

If the reply is, "Yes, I am," then the counselor can proceed this way:

"When are you the most depressed?"

"Who here depresses you the most?"

These questions let the client and the rest of the family know that depression involves relationship and sets the stage for the counselor to probe the rest of the family and find out how they operate. This can be a slow, methodical undertaking.

Probably one of the hardest lessons I have personally had to learn is that of patience. I am impulsive by nature, and I love to spring ahead and anticipate answers and formulate problems well in advance of the flow of the session. I now consciously attempt to move slowly and precisely, asking questions and observing the action as it unfolds.

During this questioning a counselor should not be afraid to be perplexed. In fact, perplexity can be a very strong position to work from: "Now forgive me, I sometimes take a long time to understand things. Mother, you said that Johnny is shouting at you all the time and that Father never comes to your assistance. But I'm still foggy on whether or not you have asked Father for help with Johnny."

If the counselor doesn't understand the problem in the first session, he tells them he doesn't know what's going on and needs to talk with them again to find out the problem. When he thinks he has a few pieces of what is happening, the counselor can test the accuracy of his hunches with the family.

While questioning the family, the counselor should always be aware of the drama unfolding before him. At times he may diverge from the questioning to follow the drama that is there. As he joins in the drama, he doesn't challenge the procedures at that point. His objective is to find out how the family carry on their business. To a degree this can be explained by the family members as he asks them questions, but much of it must also be observed as it transpires before him.

The final stage of the first interview is the resolution. This usually takes the last ten minutes. The counselor makes an assessment of the situation as he sees it at that point. As mentioned earlier, he may really have little to say regarding the situation thus far. It is very important, however, that he make some assessment, even if it is "Gee, this family is confusing." He can then explain what elements are leaving him confused.

It is usually essential for the counselor not to decide exactly what the problem is too quickly. If he knows with certainty what is happening, he will try to frame it in his mind. To speak out too quickly is to invite resistance from the family.

If the counselor does relate his understanding of the problem and the family resist, he may have to disregard that position temporarily and just pace the family for a while. Initially it is best for him not to insist that he thinks he can identify the problem. Families need to be brought along at a comfortable speed. The counselor also needs to allow himself time to evaluate his assumptions.

After the assessment the counselor contracts with the family to see if they are willing to come back. He then recommends that they come a certain number of sessions—usually at least five—at which time the contract can be renegotiated. It is critical that counselors guard their time. To do this, clear contracts are absolutely essential.

## Ongoing Counseling

It is hoped that in the first interview the counselor has established in his own mind what he is working to change in the family, with whom, and for how long (at least until the contract is renewed).

Each week as the family arrives, the counselor should go through the three stages of counseling again, taking a short social time, establishing where they are with the problem at this time, and reassessing which direction to take for next week.

Probably the most important thought for a counselor to keep in mind during his work is "What am I attempting to change?" Remember what we have said so far. In working with families we strive for second-order change—the reordering of relationships with its accompanying transformation of perspective, a restructuring of the family and individual maps. The task sounds monumental, and indeed it is.

Amazing, however, is that frequently a small change in one relationship will have devastating effects throughout the family. The counselor does not have to change everything in everyone. With this in mind, he can be comfortable working toward small changes between people and waiting for the changes to permeate the whole family. Here are some changes that one counselor has targeted:

- Have a father and mother talk with each other uninterrupted about what discipline they want for their children (when they have violently disagreed and have been perpetually interrupted).
- Have a single parent finally say something definitively about rules to a wayward teenager (when she has "waffled" for years.)
- Have a family cry about the death of a father (whose passing was never mourned).
- Have a husband take his wife's hand fifteen minutes each night and tell her his struggles (when he has always been the "strong one," never revealing his feelings to her).

Obviously many of the changes the counselor wants to initiate involve homework, in which the family must go home and work on some project, no matter how small. Homework is an excellent way of having the family "take the counselor home with them" by way of his directives.

A counselor becomes uncomfortable when he seems to reach an impasse with a family. That situation comes when all his hypotheses lead to dead ends. When he becomes frustrated with a family, he can request help from a colleague or two. Perhaps several counselors could meet regularly to review the cases. I am aware of one such group that often invites families in so that all three counselors can work on the family and learn together.

## Summary

When a counselor finally faces a family and everyone begins to talk, he may find himself completely overwhelmed and confused by the barrage of information. The counselor must be careful in structuring interviews so that he will be able to get the information he needs to make the proper interventions.

While setting the stage, the counselor must also be assured that the necessary people are present during initial sessions so that all perspectives are represented. During the first interview it is important to make contact and gain rapport with everyone rapidly. Then the counselor needs to ask questions and watch the unfolding drama as he begins to construct hypotheses about what the problem is and what needs to change.

Above all, the counselor must be patient and not rush to judgment too quickly. Relationships are complex.

## Notes

[1] Richard Fisch, John Weakland, and Lynn Segal, *The Tactics of Change* (San Francisco: Jossey-Bass, 1982), 59.

[2] Ibid., 60ff. 89ff.

[3] Ibid., 89ff.

[4] Ibid.

[5] Some of these questions come from Cloe Madanes, *Strategic Family Therapy* (San Francisco: Jossey-Bass, 1981), 117–18.

# 10
# Blending

The last generation has seen a dramatic shift in family demographics. Years ago it was assumed that all families would consist of mother, father, and children. Now, with the prevalence of divorce and second marriages, families are assembled in a variety of combinations; congregations have increasing numbers of single parents and spouses in second and third marriages. Children find themselves living with only one parent or with stepparents and stepsiblings. These family situations demand attention from counselors, ministers, and educators—all who work with families. In this chapter we will discuss single parenting and reconstituted, or blended, families.

### Single-Parent Families

In recent years family counselors have been faced with an increasing number of single-parent-family problems. I have struggled to help keep many marriages together, and then I have had to watch helplessly as these marriages have been torn apart, leaving only shattered dreams and bitterness behind. As I have worked with marriages and seen this happen, I have been quick to point out to the separating couple that it is essential that they come to terms with parenting issues apart from their marital issues. I've told them, no matter what you do with each other, you will always be these children's parents. Unfortunately, this is easier said than done.

Knowingly or unknowingly, parents often use their children as pawns in their ongoing disputes with each other. Because of this, counselors try to warn parents on the verge of divorce as to what will happen if they cannot find a way to separate their children from their marital struggles and to support each other as parents. Counselors can bluntly tell them things such as this:

> You two have unfortunately chosen to divorce. I am sorry for this. But now you must come to terms with your children. Divorce is devastating to children even under the best of conditions, when parents are somewhat amicable toward each other. The two of you must come together for their sakes, and agree on guidelines as to how they are to be raised, with common goals and expectations. If you cannot do this, it is very likely your children will eventually see (or need to see) endless therapists who will only be marginally effective. Your money will end up in the hands of attorneys. The legacy you pass on will be one of bitterness.

Tragically, such warnings are largely ignored. Warring spouses often cannot see beyond their bitterness. Consequently, over the years many counselors have become less patient with parents who exploit their children to wage battle against a spouse.

Counselors, like marriage mediators, usually try to convince divorcing couples to work out some arrangement that will be in the children's best interest and will be endorsed by both parents. This arrangement would include an agreement to keep communication open regarding parenting issues, disciplinary guidelines, and expectations about values.

It is sad that in many instances, the divorcing parents have already fought hopelessly over these issues for years. Sometimes, of course, parenting issues were a major factor in bringing them to the divorce court. But even when facing the likelihood of limited success, family counselors should attempt to reach some consensus before the couple finalizes a divorce.

Divorcing parents should be urged to tell their children jointly what they have decided to do and how this will affect the children. Parents may do this in the counselor's office with his help. Young children can be and will feel helpless; they need to know what is going to happen to them.

After couples divorce, a single-parent family is established. In these families at least two major difficulties develop that cause them to seek counseling. One has to do with hierarchy, the question of who is in charge. The second has to do with boundaries, the question of identity of the members.

*Hierarchy Situations in Single-Parent Families*

Consider the problems surrounding hierarchy. Families function most effectively when there is a clear hierarchy and everyone knows who is in charge. Single-parent families are rife with difficulties in this matter. For many of these families the counselor will not have had prior contact with the couple before they divorced. He is usually contacted by a custodial parent who is having difficulty with one or more of the children. Among the first facts he will want to know about the family is "Where is the ex-spouse and have these two parents been able to establish a mutual pattern of authority (an effective hierarchy) for the children?"

Children begin to have difficulties when the hierarchy is not clear. Parents usually have at least some trouble agreeing on how the children will be reared after the divorce. These problems can become monumental.

Two counselors writing about single parenting state that many couples obtain a legal divorce without ever achieving an emotional divorce.[1] As the battles continue, the hope of establishing effective leadership for the children is all but lost. In assessing single-parent situations when the children are acting poorly, the counselor needs to know how the divorced parents are getting along. Have they been able to arrive at common goals for the children? Have they made a complete break from each other emotionally, or are they still very much engaged with one another, possibly fighting through the children?

When a counselor works with a parent who is legally divorced but emotionally "undivorced," he should try to get both ex-spouses together so he can observe the dynamics between them. The parent who initially contacted the counselor may be horrified at this suggestion; he or she may complain that the fighting has gone on for years and that such a meeting would be distasteful, dangerous, and unproductive. The counselor can explain that until the former spouses can sit down and come to terms with each other and agree on the management of the children, there is little he can do to help the child who is doing badly. Many times his interventions as a counselor will end there. If he cannot persuade the two people to work on the problems together, he may feel compelled to drop the case.

I feel that many counselors, including myself on occasion, have stayed involved in counseling situations where our ability to contribute toward meaningful change has long since passed, or maybe never really existed. He said he has contacted ex-spouses, usually in writing, to invite them in to discuss the children. He makes it clear that they will not go back over old marital issues, because some spouses see these sessions as an opportunity for some belated marital counseling. The focus will be on the children and how each parent can manage them more effectively. He usually makes it clear that if he cannot have both parents help him, he will not stay involved in the case. Sometimes he ends with a statement of his assessment of the situation:

> "Mr. Jones, I see a very dire pattern emerging with your son. He needs the guidance and support of both parents. If you and Mary can't agree on how he is to be raised, things will probably get worse for him."

When both parents are present, the counselor can determine where they agree and disagree about the children. If there are disagreements, have these gone on for a long time? Are these two people still intensely locked into disputes reaching into the past? If so, the counselor can tell them that their struggle is spilling over into their roles as parents, and he can offer to counsel them.

If the parents are willing to talk, the counselor can try to lay to rest the issues over which they still battle. He insists that he will not see their children alone and that as the parents they must try to come to terms with each other so that they can more adequately meet their children's needs.

The counselor does not want counseling in such a situation to be a substitute for an absent parent. In some situations, divorced parents find it difficult to set limits, fearing that the children have already been through "too much" in the divorce. Noncustodial parents often become "weekend Santa Clauses," indulging the children when they have visitation rights and discarding their responsibilities to discipline the children. The custodial parent is then cast in the role of the "bad guy," with the noncustodial parent wearing the white hat.

Either the custodial or the noncustodial parents can feel guilty and as a result overindulge the children because of past hurts. These people need to know that this strategy for solving problems only exacerbates the children's pain. Setting limits is a normal, healthy process that must occur for young people to grow up feeling secure and acting responsibly.

This parental guilt can be especially marked when the marriage has been severed by the death of one spouse. The surviving parent, realizing that the children have suffered greatly because of the loss, may be quite hesitant to be firm with limits. He or she may also have aborted efforts by their children to mourn the death adequately.

A family counselor worked with a man who was having trouble with his two teenaged daughters. His wife had committed suicide several years earlier after the birth of their third daughter. The father had never talked with the girls about their mother's death and its implications for the family. He had never displayed his own grief to his daughters, hoping to be "strong" for them. Sadly, no one in the family had had an adequate mourning. The counselor provided the family an opportunity for this. He had them bring pictures of the mother and talk about what she had meant to everyone; then he simply let the whole family cry over their loss. In the process he learned that one of the girls feared that when she got older, she would get depressed and commit suicide as her mother did.

*Boundaries in Single-Parent Families*

A second major problem that leads single-parent families into counseling involves *boundaries*. Remember that boundaries between subgroups in the family must remain firm for the family to function properly. Boundary problems easily develop when one parent is present.

The most common boundary problem is called the "parentification" of a child. This simply means that one child is made a "parent" in the family, and it can happen in a number of ways. The single parent who is away a lot might give the oldest child responsibility for the younger children. This situation can be healthy only if the child is mature enough, is given appropriate and limited responsibilities, and is granted some power to fulfill them.

Problems develop when a child is given responsibility with little or no power to carry out the task. Many children—some as young as eight—have told one counselor that they go to sleep at night worrying about their mothers and their younger siblings, because they feel it is their sole responsibility to care for all these people. Anxiety builds in these children as they see difficulties developing in their families over which they have no control, yet feel responsible for. In such situations the counselor should talk with the parent and the children to clarify the responsibilities.

Another boundary problem arises when the single parent confides all his or her worries and concerns to a child. In some cases the parent is leaning on the child for emotional support and is giving information far beyond that child's capabilities to assimilate it.

One counselor tells of working with a teenaged girl who listened to all her mother's problems, helped shop for her mother's clothes, and generally guided her mother through life. This girl was worried because she was preparing to graduate from high school and go away to college. She was sincerely concerned that her mother would not be able to function in the world without her.

The counselor tried to release the child from parenting the parent and to find other options for the mother. Often the parent has been cut off from wholesome adult relationships because of work and home responsibilities. It becomes essential for such parents to connect themselves with helpful persons, possibly their own age, who can begin to meet their needs and balance their lives in wholesome ways.

In another case, the counselor worked with a single mother and her two teenaged girls. As he talked with them, it appeared as though he were talking with three sisters. He began to support the mother *as* a mother and to bolster her in her role as parent, giving her guidelines for dealing more appropriately with her daughters.

## The Blended Family

Frequently we now see blended families in which a mother and a father from different marriages have come together, bringing along several children. After working with such families, it became apparent to me that someone cannot just assemble people in this manner and expect the group all of a sudden to live like a natural family.

Blending two families is hard on everyone in different ways. The new husband and wife need time to become a "we." This is best done when the two have only each other and focus on getting to know one another. However, when there are children requiring care, the marriage relationship frequently lacks the attention it deserves.

The children desire attention from their natural parent and may resent the presence of a stepparent who represents another demand on the parent's time. Battles erupt over who has had the most time with the parent. Parents feel caught in hopeless loyalty disputes between children and new spouses.

### Wanting Affection

One type of problem in blended families is the "affection" problem. Stepparents come on the scene and immediately expect stepchildren to embrace them with open arms. This rarely happens, even after a long, fairly amicable engagement. Loyalty is the issue. Children feel loyal to their natural parents—even those who are deceased—and feel like traitors if they give affection to a stepparent.

Natural parents and stepparents who try to force love and loyalty from their children usually face a great deal of resistance. "You can't make me love you" is a true statement. Love takes time to grow. Children need to learn that love is not quantitative; giving love to one person does not diminish how much is left for another.

Unfortunately, many adults feel intensely rejected as they fail to experience love coming from stepchildren. Then they go overboard trying to win affection, only to find themselves in worse condition than when they started.

### Problems of Authority

A second type of problem in blended families has to do with issues of authority—that is, hierarchy. Breakdowns in authority can come from many quarters. Ideally the new parents need to establish their authority as quickly as possible so that they can present a united front to all family members. Several factors can hinder this from happening.

Many parents feel loyalty first to their natural children and in fact take their side against the stepparent when conflict arises. Families sometimes split right down the middle along biological lines, the father and his natural children against the mother and her natural children. In such cases a counselor needs to work only with the parents, telling them they have to reach a consensus on how their family will be run.

Authority is often undermined by people who are not on the scene. The most familiar culprit is the ex-spouse, who consciously or unconsciously may desire that the new family fail. Often when children visit this natural parent, they are enticed to criticize the stepparent. Sometimes the former spouse will actually encourage children to disobey the stepparent.

When a natural parent on the outside interferes this way, the counselor should contact the person about discussing with the new couple the difficulties of raising the children. He can emphasize that if a consensus cannot be reached, the children will be the ones to suffer the most. If the person is uncooperative, there is little the counselor can do besides warning the ex-spouse that unless the outside interference is stopped, the children will continue to suffer and in all likelihood will get worse.

Sometimes interference comes from a grandparent opposed to the new union. Many grandparents wittingly or unwittingly endorse the misbehavior of their grandchildren in stepparenting situations. Again, these grandparents should be contacted and asked to cooperate with the parents in keeping the children on the right path.

Some authority problems begin to develop with stepparents who confuse affection with authority: "If I come down too hard on my stepchildren, they will never love me." Consequently the stepparent backs off and a clear hierarchy is never established.

A third type of problem within blended families is "turf." These problems are especially acute when one spouse moves into a house previously occupied by the other spouse. This is a particularly bad idea, because personal space is a big issue in families anyway. The issue intensifies when a stepparent comes into a home where turf has already been established; problems can erupt quickly.

A counselor worked with a remarried woman who had a ten-year-old daughter. She and the daughter moved into her husband's home, where there were already two teenaged daughters. The man had lived in this home with his first wife, who had died, then with his daughters for a number of years. The teenaged girls did not want to relinquish the kitchen to their father's new wife. They felt this woman was intruding on their space, and they wouldn't give an inch.

It is always best, though it is not always possible, for newly blended families to move into a new home where no one has any predetermined space. Then the mother and father can begin to mark out the space.

## Summary

The shape of the American family has changed drastically in the last generation. More single-parent families and blended families populate the country than ever before. Each situation makes unique demands on family members, causing various pressures and problems that can lead these families to seek help from counselors.

In a single-parent family it is important to determine if a divorce has been completed emotionally as well as legally. Despite the divorce, the natural parents must learn to pull together to raise the children in harmony. Single parents must keep proper boundaries between themselves and their children so the children can be free to be young.

When single parents marry, there is a blending of families, creating stepparents and stepchildren. Parents cannot simply join formerly separate families and expect the group suddenly to work like a natural family. Stepparents need to go slow in expecting affection. Clear lines of authority must be quickly established, with all concerned adults—including ex-spouses and grandparents—endorsing the leadership.

## Notes

[1] Anita Morawetz and Gillian Walker, *Brief Therapy With Single-Parent Families* (New York: Brunner/Mazel, 1984).

# 11
# Thinking

Now Abel kept flocks, and Cain worked the soil. In the course of time Cain brought some of the fruits of the soil as an offering to the LORD. But Abel brought fat portions from some of the firstborn of his flock. The LORD looked with favor on Abel and his offering, but on Cain and his offering he did not look with favor. So Cain was very angry, and his face was downcast.

Then the LORD said to Cain, "Why are you angry? Why is your face downcast? If you do what is right, will you not be accepted? But if you do not do what is right, sin is crouching at your door; it desires to have you, but you must master it."

Now Cain said to his brother Abel, "Let's go out to the field." And while they were in the field, Cain attacked his brother Abel and killed him (Gen. 4:2–8).

Even the first human family had major problems and faced disaster. Envy and sibling rivalry exploded into murder. Families have experienced problems ever since. The need for wise counsel and intervention has always been present.

We have talked about how families are organized, how they carry on the business of living, and how a counselor can spot difficulties and move to make corrections as problems develop. I would like to relate several actual cases that illustrate the principles of family counseling presented in this book. The summaries show how I conceptualized problems and made interventions.

*1: The Case of the Missing Minds*

A fifteen-year-old boy was brought to me by his parents. The mother had scheduled the appointment. She proved to be the one who orchestrated most of the boy's life. He was currently attending a special school for children with learning disabilities. He had been adopted at a very early age.

The parents reported and the school confirmed that the boy was socially very immature, had few friends, was doing very poorly in school, and had begun to talk back to his teachers. His mother was concerned that he had a "poor self-image" and to her way of thinking he had basically given up on life.

The boy was the oldest of three children. He had a twelve-year-old sister, also adopted, and a ten-year-old brother who was the natural child of the parents. The fifteen-year-old was somewhat overweight, but seemed normal in other respects.

As I talked with the family during the first session, the mother seemed to answer every question. She was particularly effective at explaining everyone to me. When the boy expressed some rather negative feelings about his dad, the mother was there to defend her husband as being excellent in every way. The boy immediately backed off.

In cases of adoption where the child is having problems with esteem, investigation often discloses that for some reason he has been treated "special" by the parents and because of this he is never able to feel that he fits into the family like everyone else. This can be confusing, because it appears that his being adopted causes all the distress. In reality not the adoption, but the special treatment is the cause. So in this case I sought to find out how this family had treated the boy "special."

It turned out that both parents—especially the mother—had struggled with the boy all through school because of his learning deficiencies. His siblings had continually moaned about his special treatment and their feeling neglected. As we talked I began to develop the frame I would present to the family: "This boy has never *fit* in this family! What's more, he always feels deprived because of all that you parents have attempted to give him!"

The mother didn't perceive fully what I meant by "deprived," and she didn't like what little she did understand. As we talked further, I found that whenever the boy said he felt bored, the mother would try to entertain him. Whenever he was late for dinner, the mother would delay it for him—much to the displeasure of his father. When the boy came home from school, his mother would check his homework assignments and then proceed with a litany of nagging to make sure he finished it.

I decided to add to my frame: "Mother has taken this boy's mind and memory. And along with these two, she has also managed to take away his responsibility." By then I had the father in my court; he understood what I meant. I said this in such a way as to let the mother know that I was not condemning her, but was seeking to understand her struggles.

I pressed on to find out why she would deny the boy (and also his sister) nothing. I learned that the mother came from a very deprived background where material things and affection were sorely lacking and spread among ten children. Whenever she saw her children feeling bad, she saw her own childhood of deprivation and sprang into action. Her solution became the problem, however, for the more she was there to fill her children's needs, to anticipate their wants, and to take over their responsibilities, the more she chipped away at their sense of self. People develop healthy senses of themselves by planning, executing, failing, and pushing ahead until they succeed.

The next task was for me to convince the parents of this truth and to assure them that I did not condemn these heroic efforts while trying to persuade them to alter their approach in the future. I planned with the parents how to back out of the boy's life so he could learn how to make his own decisions and to fail when he made errors. First, I told the mother she would have to give him back his mind and memory; he might resist this, and he would probably have to fail for a while until he realized that his parents would not be there to continually bail him out and take over his responsibilities.

When the mother returned the next week, she was worried. She realized that if she gave her son back his mind and quit taking responsibility for him, she would essentially be out of a job and would have much empty time on her hands. Having recognized this, she immediately began to think about working outside the home.

I worked with the family for about six months, never really deviating from the frames I have defined. The tendency was for the boy to begin failing at school, thus activating the mother to come to his rescue. I helped the family through several of these crises until I felt comfortable that the mother was sufficiently permitting the boy to fail periodically.

The problem of taking responsibility for and away from another person occurs frequently and not always between parent and child.

In one marital counseling situation, the wife wanted me to change her husband because, she said, "he is so irresponsible." He had waited until his early thirties to get married. He found himself married to a very strong woman, who knew her mind definitively on every subject. As the couple came together in marriage, he found himself more and more surrendering his reasoning powers to her. At the same time, he was less and less willing to argue his point of view.

Of course, the less he did, the more she did. Both of them expected him to do less and her to do more. She berated him for his irresponsibility. He retreated, and felt less and less important in his family. Whenever he was with his wife, he literally put his mind on Hold and let her make all the decisions.

In a case like this, obviously, the task of the counselor is to get the "mindless" person functioning again and making personal decisions. It was very difficult for me to get the man activated while having his wife step back a little to give him room to exercise his reasoning capacities. What worked best with the couple was to make the whole procedure into a game in which he was to make one decision each day that the wife had to go along with—a decision that he was quite able to make.

## 2: The Case of the Life in Shambles

A middle-aged divorcée whom we'll call Sara came to me because she saw her life in shambles. Her children were living with her ex-husband. She was underemployed and marginally involved in school to help update her credentials. She did not seem to have a clue as to what her life should look like. She was a Christian and active in her church. Apparently a number of church friends had been mobilized to give her plenty of advice. She was obviously intelligent and talented, and I knew that giving more advice was not the answer to the problems.

I asked myself, "What keeps Sara from straightening out her life?" Instead of asking her this question, I decided to ask her, "*Who* keeps you from straightening out your life?" Sara immediately answered that it was her paternal grandmother. I asked if she would need to ask permission of her grandmother to straighten out her life. She said yes. The way I framed my questions to her may seem strange, but when different generations are involved in counseling, hidden loyalties appear that are passed down from one generation to another, almost like a bad debt. From the way she answered, it appeared that she owed someone "failure," and this debt would have to be satisfied.

I probed into Sara's family background to see what that might yield. (I normally don't go on archaeological expeditions unless I am after something in particular.) I discovered that Sara's mother and father had repeatedly separated during the years of their marriage. Her father had never really separated from *his* mother, and when he and his wife would separate, he would always head home. In fact, he was still alive and currently living with his mother at the time I was counseling his daughter.

Sara had spent a great deal of her growing years living with her paternal grandparents. When she was at her grandparents' home, she would sleep with her grandmother while the grandfather slept in a different room. The grandmother was always angry toward Sara's mother, and Sara was drawn into the struggle on grandmother's side.

In Sara's mother's family, women were demeaned and subservient and considered incompetent. Men were catered to constantly. Sara had an older brother who thus received most parental accolades and was expected to succeed in all he did. Most of what Sara did never really counted for much. When she failed at anything, it had been expected by her parents.

But there was one arena in which Sara had succeeded while her brother had failed: she had produced much-coveted grandchildren, whereas he had not. Indeed, his life was not the smashing success it was supposed to be. It was unthinkable that Sara would outshine her brother, for that was just not done in that family.

So Sara was in the middle of many relationships. She was

between her paternal grandmother and her mother (and allied with her grandmother). She was therefore drawn in on her father's side against her mother and in the middle of their fights. And she was also in a triangle between her brother and her parents. She was mighty important in a negative way to many people. I surmised that if she succeeded and got on with her own life, many people in her family might collapse, not having her around to act as a buffer.

A person in the middle of so many relationships acts as a buffer and in that way protects the members of the family. If this restraining force is removed, open conflict tends to erupt. Sara knew that to be loyal she had to fail, and fail she did. So I gave her this frame: "Your failure maintains many people. Can you afford, or can they afford, to have you succeed at this time?"

I let her think about this for a month. I knew I had put a lot on her to contemplate. She returned in a month to say that she was unsure whether she was ready to make the giant step from failure to success. I told her that timing was important and this should not be rushed. I then let her go for another two months, merely warning her to "go slow."

She returned in two months to say that she was back in school and had found the occupational directives she needed. She had taken steps to change aspects of her social and family life that needed adjustment. I was amazed that she had done so much. I was also perplexed as to what factors had brought about all this activity. All she would say was that she gave me most of the credit.

### 3: The Case of the Lack of Problems

A mother and father were concerned about their thirteen-year-old son. The mother told me over the phone that she was not sure there really was a problem, but wanted me to take a look. Each year I receive several calls like this, where the problem is ill-defined.

The first session was an energy drain for me as I poked around trying to see who was anxious and for what reasons. No one seemed particularly concerned about anything. The father stated that the boy had not done as well in school as he should have, getting B's and C's. The mother stated that the boy liked to stay around the house a lot and read by himself. He did have friends, but he liked being alone. He also had a paper route at which he was most faithful, and he was active in the church youth group.

When I asked the boy if he felt he had any problems, he answered quite definitively, "No." He said he was happy with his life and saw no need to change anything.

After this interview I had the distinct sense that I was not seeing a true picture, but all my interviewing skills and questions had been expended. The next week I saw the boy alone to try to find out if, by questioning him without his parents there, I could elicit some new information. Nothing new was forthcoming. He was adamant in seeing himself as healthy.

I had been totally unsuccessful in discerning any anxiety about any problems. The supposed difficulties were discussed in a perfunctory manner. It is important, when people come to me with problems, for me to see where they are anxious and upset. As I probe the various relationships in the family, I want to see where the pain is, how the family is organized, and where I will need to do my work.

With families in which there is little or no anxiety, I feel comfortable telling them, "Now is not the time for counseling. Whatever problems there may be are not yet ready for attention."

Some people wonder why I don't try some "preventative" measures. I have found that if I am working with only my turmoil—I'm the only one concerned about the family problem!— motivation is low to nonexistent. I end up working twice as hard while the family just sits by and watches.

In this case I told the family that I saw no reason for concern at that time. If things turned bad, they were to call. I am confident that if there are real problems there, they will manifest themselves and the anxiety will significantly increase. Then I will be able to intervene more thoroughly.

4: *The Case of the Girl Who Was Out of Control, Right Between the Parents*

I do not delve into marital issues overtly unless I am invited to do so. From the time I first started counseling families, it became obvious that many children were doing poorly because of tensions between the parents. When I pointed this out to a family, I invariably met strong resistance. The family would always seem to redirect me back to the "real" problem of the child. Since then, I have moved cautiously when it comes to confronting parents with their inadequacies. I find that I can be much more effective by adhering initially to the presenting problem and working to bring about marital harmony as a corollary to the main problem.

As an example, I can have a mother and father who have agreed about very little in years work toward agreement to get a wayward child under control. I don't have to say, "Now I'm going to work on your marriage." The intervention comes much more naturally, such as saying something like, "Listen, this child is much too clever at getting between the two of you. We must now find a way to come together to get her under control."

However, a particular case was somewhat different in that, after several sessions with the family, the mother and father both admitted their need to improve their marriage. In this case, the couple brought in their daughter, a senior in high school. They were concerned because they felt they absolutely could not control her. She was dating boys her parents didn't like and doing other things they found unacceptable.

As I probed, I learned that the mother had been very close to this girl in a negative way all of her life. From her birth the girl was regarded by her mother as "strong-willed." The girl in turn was never happy with her mother. Consequently a pattern was established early in which the mother tried to do the right thing by her daughter, but always sensed she failed. Struggles ensued between them. Meanwhile, the father was busy in his career and basically uninvolved.

As we talked during several sessions, it became clear that the mother felt chronically alone and isolated from her husband. She was able to verbalize this very clearly. The father also expressed his discontent. At this point I dismissed the daughter and asked the parents if they wished to pursue their marriage problems; they said they did. I elected to hold the girl's difficulties in abeyance, since she appeared not to be in very much danger, and turned my attention to the parents' marriage.

We worked on the marriage successfully for several months. But it was very difficult at times to keep to this agenda. When the daughter did something irregular, the parents tended to revert to the former agenda and forget the marriage problems.

It is always important to stay as focused as possible regarding what problems you are working on and with whom.

## 5: The Case of the Unfinished Painting

A mother and father brought their sixteen-year-old son to me, because even though he was extremely bright, he was not doing well in school. He had a poor self-image, was probably depressed, and argued endlessly with his parents about everything imaginable. He rebelled against most forms of authority and generally refused to accept the consequences of his actions, blaming others for his various failures. The mother felt that the father was too soft in his handling of the boy. The father thought the mother was too harsh.

This case took many months to unfold fully. The more I pursued, the more the path led to new areas of inquiry.

My initial agenda with the family was to attempt to get the boy back under some sort of control, with both parents agreeing on boundaries and consequences for him. I asked these questions first: Who gives him permission to argue so much with his mother and father? Who is he most like? Who tore out his self-esteem, and how? How come he gets away with so much? The parents never carry through; why not?

As we discussed these questions, I discovered that the mother had a low-grade, chronic depression. The father drank excessively. Seven years earlier he had taken a year off from work to write a book. That year had stretched into seven without yielding much writing at all. The mother had been working to augment his military retirement pay. The father appeared to be the one who always bailed the boy out of his failures. I initially framed the father this way: "You have lost your place since you left the service."

It seemed to me that both parents regarded their son in some special way that prohibited them from acting decisively with him. I wanted to find out why the father was always bailing out the boy. The father had always noted the boy's depression and had feared suicide. Two very close friends of his had died when he was young—one from suicide—and he had always felt guilty that he might have been able to do more for them. Now he was in a panic over his son. His only solution to the problem was to indulge the boy and rescue him from all his difficulties, fearing that if he did not, he might somehow "push him over the edge." Truly, the solution had become the problem. My frame to the father was this: "You subsidize your son's irresponsibility."

The mother, by contrast, stayed too close to her son because she felt all his life that she had had a gifted, bright child and had never been quite able to complete the job of adequately raising him and preparing him for life. Consequently she nagged and picked at him to do better—causing him to rebel against her even more. Interestingly, though this woman had been a model child, her own mother had thought she rebelled as did her son now. The mother felt that she had perpetually let her own mother down, even though she had achieved much in her life. This was my frame to the mother: "You look at your son and always see an unfinished painting that you are frantically trying to complete before he leaves forever."

I decided to take a two-pronged approach. First, I would get the mother and father together so they could for once have a coordinated plan of attack with their child. Second, I would get their son under some sort of control with the mother and father acting as competent parents. I saw the parents alone and framed them this way: "You have both become stuck over the past seven years, and your 'stuckness' can be summed up in the phrase 'If only. . . .'" For the father, "if only" was in getting a job when he retired from the service or in finishing his book. For the mother, "if only" was in going back to work and leaving her kids. I told them to separately make "if only" lists, read them to each other, and then burn the lists in the fireplace.

My main goal was to move the boy out of the center of everyone's attention. As I told the parents, this boy could not walk through the living room without drawing the attention from either or both parents. They both were particularly fond of "lecturing," which was profoundly ineffective with their son.

Slowly, with much encouragement, the parents were able to back off from the boy, set proper limits, and move him in the proper direction. As the issues with the boy decreased, issues with the mother and father increased. They asked if they could now work on their marriage. I was happy to do this with them, since my work with their son was basically completed.

Frequently, as a counselor is successful getting problems

solved with children in a family, problems will emerge between the parents. As in the previous case, it is important to keep agendas clear. Families with problems tend to have problems with boundaries, children getting between parents and operating in ways they shouldn't. It is crucial for the counselor to reestablish clear boundaries. If the counselor works on marriages with children present, boundaries remain fuzzy.

### 6: *The Case of the Terrible Fears*

A mother brought me a ten-year-old girl who was having fears of falling, being chased, and being hurt. These fears would stay with her a long time, upsetting the parents. The girl had been a compulsive handwasher—a compulsion in which a person washes his or hands a great deal, feeling that they are always dirty.

These fears had started right before the beginning of the school term the last two years. The father in particular had become alarmed. When his daughter had begun reporting the fears, the father rallied the whole family to find out all that she was thinking and fearing. He had insisted on counseling to find out what was the matter.

In this kind of a case with a child of this age, my concern is that the symptom might become crystallized so that the child is labeled as sick and placed in extended counseling. Discussing a symptom of this nature is seductive in that a great deal of information can be gathered and the child and family can be quizzed endlessly about what is happening. But I try to move this type of case out of my office very quickly with a minimum of intervention.

I noted that everyone in the family had become involved in discussing the girl's symptoms with her. I decided to call a halt to this. I said that for the next two weeks I did not want anyone to discuss her fears. If she brought up a new fear, the mother or father should write it down, but definitely not discuss it with her. My thought was that possibly the overemphasis on the problems by the family was fostering the situation.

After two weeks the fears were completely gone and, with follow-up, never recurred. I also did not see the family again. There are several issues that I did not explore, but which appeared to be present. First, the father favored the girl and evidently indulged her. Second, the mother and father disagreed on discipline, the mother being the harsher. Third, the children worried about the tensions between their parents. These issues could certainly have been explored, but the family only wanted the fears in the daughter to be gone. Once they were gone, motivation for further counseling ended. My thinking is that even though I might see such problems operating in a family and needing attention, I want the family to ask me to deal with them.

### Conclusion

In all the hundreds of families that I have seen over the years, two things still amaze me: that I am much harder on myself and my performance than families are on me, and that God can take our mistakes and feeble attempts to help and still weave his purposes.

More often than not, when I feel as though I have failed, either I have missed the point of what was going on in the family or I was unable to execute proper interventions; yet, from the ashes of that seeming defeat has come change. I now realize that change frequently comes about in spite of me, not because of me. Because of this, I find myself more relaxed, more able to ride the bumps with the family, and not feeling the pressure to work instant wonders.

# Afterword

Relationship is like the air. It is all around us. It sustains us. We can sense its presence and especially its absence. But few of us take the time to notice. Even though relationship is essential to our well-being, few of us consider its nature, trace its path, or alter its course.

We have taken the time in this book to consider the nature of the family relationship. We have seen how very critical family interactions can be in the development and maintenance of problems. We must never forget that family relationships lie at the basis of all other relationships and that the healthy continuation of these relationships is critical to our survival.

Obviously this has not been an exhaustive study. It is intended as an introduction, an attempt to recalibrate ways of understanding people and their problems, a summons to stop and take note of this critical aspect of life. Even as I write, I stop for a moment and take notice of the air conditioning that is now blowing into my room. I had not noticed it before, but I had enjoyed its benefits. If a problem now developed in the room temperature, it would become critical that I know more about the functioning of the system or find someone who does.

Most of us who have counseled have known the frustration and perplexity in this profession. The webs that keep people bound can be complex. Perplexity can be a chronic condition. It is hoped that as those engaged in counseling have read these pages, there have been new insights forged and new paths of inquiry designated.

I do not pretend to be certain about these concepts. Much of my thinking of relationship is in transition, being ever remolded with new learning and observations. But that is precisely what makes Christian counseling exciting. We are anchored to the Rock, knowing that he created us and sustains us and ultimately holds all truth, while at the same time we venture forth into new lines of investigation in an attempt to better understand all that he has made.

# Index

*178*